Ministry with
Families in Flux

Ministry with Families in Flux

The Church and Changing Patterns of Life

Richard P. Olson
and
Joe H. Leonard, Jr.

WESTMINSTER/JOHN KNOX PRESS
Louisville, Kentucky

Scripture quotations from the Revised Standard Version of the Bible are copyrighted 1946, 1952, © 1971, 1973 by the Division of Christian Education of the National Council of the Churches of Christ in the U.S.A. and are used by permission.

Book design by Polebridge Press, Inc.

First edition

Published by Westminster/John Knox Press
Louisville, Kentucky

PRINTED IN THE UNITED STATES OF AMERICA

9   8   7   6   5   4   3   2   1

Library of Congress Cataloging-in-Publication Data

Olson, Richard P.
    Ministry with families in flux : the church and changing patterns of life / Richard P. Olson and Joe H. Leonard, Jr. — 1st ed.
        p.   cm.
    Includes bibliographical references.
    ISBN 0–664–25082–3

    1. Church work with families—United States. 2. Family—United States. 3. Family—Religious life. I. Leonard, Joe H. II. Title.
BV4438.047 1990
259'.1—dc20   89-48566
                                                                CIP

Contents

Acknowledgments   vii

1. A Perspective on the Changing Family   3

2. The Effect of Changing Employment Patterns   22

3. The Single-Parent Family   40

4. Images of Remarried Families   59

5. Religious or Value Differences   76

6. Couples Without Children   96

7. Issues of Space and Time   115

8. Families with Members Who Have Disabilities   132

9. Diversities of Family Membership   152

10. The Caring Church's Response   172

Acknowledgments

Dick expresses thanks to the people in the churches he has served. These folk have shared the joys and struggles of their varied family lives. In recent years a good number have graciously allowed him to conduct information-gathering interviews with them.

Joe thanks the parents related to the Greater Philadelphia Chapter of the Autism Society of America for conversation and insight. He also thanks his colleagues on the Commission on Family Ministries and Human Sexuality of the National Council of the Churches of Christ and the Pennsylvania Developmental Disabilities Planning Council for continuing to challenge him.

Thanks are due also to a wide number of pastoral colleagues, lay church leaders, and family-life professionals and organizations, a few of whom are quoted by name, most of whom are not. We have sent out mail inquiries, conducted clergy listening groups, and talked family ministry with colleagues where we met them; we appreciate their unselfish sharing of successes and unsolved dilemmas.

A special word of thanks is extended to Dr. Ruth Hatch, adjunct professor of family life, Central Baptist Theological Seminary. Ruth provided bibliography, did library research, offered leads to persons with insights about various family types, and evaluated chapters in progress. She also used several chapters as a text for her seminary class "American Family Lifestyles" and requested chapter-by-chapter critiques from class members. We appreciate their suggestions as well.

And we extend our gratitude to Harold Twiss, who, on behalf of Westminster/John Knox Press, evaluated our proposal and saw it through to completion.

Ministry with
Families in Flux

1

A Perspective on the Changing Family

We write on behalf of the changing American family. Our belief is that the church can vitally serve the wide diversity of family types in our society. It can also help families adjust to changes yet to come. We believe this will be a marvelous extension of the mission of the church. In turn, changing families will enrich the life of the church immeasurably.

At present, opinion is mixed regarding the dialogue between church and changing families. Some families bear witness to the sensitivity their church showed them when they experienced change. However, all too few families feel this way. More often, churches that offer much to families in general become paralyzed when dealing with some of the newly evolving family types. This paralysis stems from two sources: lack of comfort with and expertise about each family type's unique dynamics and needs, and uncertainty about faith perspectives on changing families.

To respond to the first of those uncertainties, we will explore many of these changing family types and their unique needs. We will identify ministries with these family types that have been undertaken and will make suggestions for other possibilities.

However, before we do this, we need to explore some other questions. What are the facts about families in America today? How did their present situation come about? What are the Christian responses to these facts? How does one apply biblical teaching about family life to the present scene? We need both a historical perspective and a biblical-theological perspective. This chapter is our effort to provide them.

3

A Historical Perspective

A number of changes have taken place in families over the last century or two. Each is important; taken together, their impact is powerful. All these changes interact with one another, but for purposes of discussion we shall isolate them. What are these changes?

Urbanization

First of all, the family moved from the farm to the city. In 1790, the rural population (farmers and nonfarmers) of the United States was nearly 95 percent of the total population. The U.S. Census Bureau did not begin distinguishing farmers from rural nonfarmers in its reports until 1880. Their figures from that time on reveal the extent of this change. In 1880, 43.8 percent of Americans were farmers. By 1920 this had shrunk to 30.1 percent. It was 23.2 percent in 1940 and 8.7 percent in 1960 (U.S. Bureau of the Census 1975, p. 457; the full reference is listed at the end of the chapter.) By 1980 it was 3.3 percent. In two centuries, the setting for the American family changed from 95 percent rural to 97 percent predominantly urban (or at least nonfarm)! Events of the 1980s indicate that the farming population will shrink even more. Further, farming itself has changed tremendously over this period. Once a labor-intensive occupation, where the efforts of many family members were needed, farming today is a capital-intensive venture, requiring the labor of very few family members.

Changing Needs and Expectations

This leads to a second observation. The needs and expectations of family members have changed. Some family tasks and roles have evolved, some have vanished, and others have become more prominent. In those earlier farm settings, the needs, tasks, and roles of husband and wife were separate and quite definite. The man was expected to provide the raw materials for creating a home, food, and clothing. He was to protect the family. The woman was to preserve and cook food, weave and sew cloth, care for the home, and bear and raise children. For the most part, the test of an effective family was functional: Were the needed tasks for family survival performed? If so, it was a successful family (Barbeau 1971, p. 2).

Much of this had changed by the twentieth century, when persons increasingly contracted marriages for personal and emotional needs. Warm community and communication, an atmosphere for personal growth (for the couple, the family, and its individual members), a supportive emotional climate, a satisfying romantic-sexual relationship—these were some of the hopes for marriages. At the same time, it was expected that families would be places to experience personal freedom, individualism, and sexual equality. Some family functions and expectations decreased; others rose dramatically, although potential partners were offered little preparation in the interpersonal task of fulfilling such high hopes for marriage.

Self-selection of Marriage Partners

Third, the process of mate selection changed. To be more accurate, the changes that began to emerge in preceding centuries continued and accelerated. Both historically and cross-culturally, the family network had influenced or controlled the choice of marital partners for young adults. While this was already on the decline in Europe in the eighteenth and nineteenth centuries, the decline accelerated greatly on American soil (Shorter 1975, p. 65). Family influence over mate selection was offered informally, and even this waned. As time passed, more and more young adults moved away from their families of origin. Work, education, or military service took them to new settings. There they selected their own marital partners, based on friendship, compatibility, romance, and sexual attraction.

Demographic Changes

Fourth, changes in death rates and life expectancy had an impact on families. Infant and child mortality declined through the nineteenth and twentieth centuries. One study showed, for example, that a baby's chance to survive its first year rose from 80 percent in the late eighteenth century to 99 percent in the late twentieth century (Greeley 1979, p. 21). Therefore, it became less necessary for parents to have many children in order to assure the survival of a few. With growing knowledge of contraception it was possible to control fertility. Women began having fewer children and having them later.

The life expectancy of both men and women increased. For men, the expected life span increased by about fourteen years from the mid-nineteenth century to the mid-twentieth. For women, the life expectancy almost doubled (Ruether 1984, p. 29).

All these demographic facts had an impact on the family. Couples spent less of their lives together raising young children. In the late-twentieth century couples spent only 18 percent of their married life raising young children, compared to 54 percent a century before (Bane 1976, p. 25). A lifetime commitment to marriage became a bigger, longer responsibility. In the eighteenth century, a typical young couple (groom age 25 and bride age 20) had a 57 percent chance of both surviving for 25 years of marriage. By the late twentieth century, a similar-age couple had a 92 percent chance of both surviving. The average possible duration of a marriage nearly doubled from about 25 years to about 50 years (Sullivan 1979, p. 20). This meant that couples had a better chance of surviving to "empty nest" years after children had left.

Increased life expectancy also meant there were fewer orphans. (Many institutions created for orphans found it necessary to find other uses.) This also meant that more persons lived to be grandparents and to add that dimension to family life. The larger number of elderly persons in society brought about another development. Their status changed—from socially honored to burdensome on society (Greeley 1979, pp. 18ff; Bane 1976, p. 25; Ruether 1984, p. 29).

The Separation of Sex and Reproduction

Fifth, both the technology and behavior of sex changed. Sex had always had a double purpose—personal enjoyment and perpetuation of the human race. Technology separated those two purposes, at least in part.

Scientific advances promised the possibility of sexual intercourse without fear of pregnancy. To replace older, cruder methods of birth control new ones were developed. For many, the pill and the IUD increased the convenience and aesthetics of the sexual experience. There was even research into a "morning after" pill. Increasing numbers of those desiring permanent freedom from pregnancies chose tubal ligations and vasectomies. An option for those whose methods of first-line birth control failed was the legalization of abortion in 1973. Though this alternative was stridently debated and severely attacked, it was widely used. In the 1980s there were about 1.3 million abortions a year in the United States.

It must be noted that these various birth control methods and their use were far from perfect in effectiveness. In the 1980s there were a half million out-of-wedlock births a year. Most of these, according to the mothers, were unwanted and unplanned.

For a time, the effectiveness of antibiotic medicines in curing venereal diseases reduced yet other fears. This trend ended rather abruptly with the appearance of new diseases for which no cure existed. One of these, herpes, was rather mild in consequences; the other, AIDS, was not. A painful, costly illness followed by death was the grim prospect for those in whom this virus became active. Still, a good many people trusted the technology of their culture to provide safe, curable, childless sex.

At the same time, technological options were being made available for persons who desired conception without intercourse. Or, more accurately, possibilities of conception were offered to those for whom intercourse with a partner had failed to produce a pregnancy. In vitro fertilization, surrogate mothers, sperm banks, and artificial insemination offered promise to persons with problems of infertility. It was soon discovered that none of these were ideal solutions. A whole new body of law began to emerge over the rights of surrogate mothers and the persons with whom they might make contracts. While the number of persons using these options was rather small, media coverage increased public awareness and consideration of them as options.

Such changes occasioned these questions: If intercourse can be separated from conception and conception from intercourse, what is the meaning of the sexual experience? At what stage in one's life may it begin? Between whom may it take place, appropriately and responsibly? Is the decision to engage in it as serious a matter as it once was? What religious norms are available to guide us in this changed situation? What are the values that apply in this age? Historian Edward Shorter, who has studied European and American families over recent centuries, perceives a compelling drive toward liberation from the sexual controls that family and community formerly imposed on young persons. By the 1960s "the chances were very high that young people who felt attached to each other would extend their relationship into the sexual domain" (Shorter 1975, p. 119). This trend has accelerated. A Lou Harris poll in the late eighties revealed that, by age 17, 57 percent report having had intercourse.

Gains for Women

Sixth, the women's movement gained increased strength and vigor, and many values from this movement also made their impact on the family, such as the four that follow.

1. Women are not "biologically destined" to be only in the mother-homemaker role.

2. All aspects of society and all occupations should be open equally to men and women. Full development to the extent of one's potentialities should be available for all.

3. When both husband and wife are employed, there is no predetermined role prescription for the division of labor among them. Child-rearing, food preparation, and house care and maintenance should be negotiated between the couple on an equal basis.

4. All persons should be free of violence in sexual and domestic situations. Rape, incest, sexual abuse, and physical-emotional-spiritual abuse should be squarely faced. Victims should be protected and abusers detected, prosecuted, restrained, and cured, if possible.

The most widespread factor contributing to these changes was the increased presence of women in the work force. In the year 1900, 5.6 percent of all women were formally employed. This grew to 50 percent by 1975 (Stearns 1979, p. 118). It is estimated that by 1995, women will account for 60 percent of the labor force (*Wall Street Journal* 11/26/85, p. 1). The widespread presence of women outside the home brought a need for adjustment in child care arrangements, in distribution of power in the family, and in male-female roles.

Changing Views of Marriage

Seventh, organized religion and other institutions experienced diminished influence as a stabilizing influence on marriage. In the twentieth century there has evolved increasing tension between two views of the married state. Is marriage basically dedicated to the welfare and stability of society? Does it have divine blessing and divine sanctions? Or is it a private agreement between two people for their enjoyment and satisfaction? The famed Lutheran theologian and martyr Dietrich Bonhoeffer wrote from his prison cell to those contemplating marriage, "Your love is your own private possession, but marriage is more than something personal, it is a status, an office" (quoted in Barbeau 1971, p. 39). Increasingly, however, couples saw marriage as a two-person contract that could be terminated when either party desired.

Shrinking Family Size

Eighth, the average size of families decreased considerably, from 5.76 children per family in the late nineteenth century to 3.06 in the 1970s (Bane 1976, p. 45). By 1986 the U.S. Census Bureau reported that the size of the average household—adults and children living together—was 2.71 people, the lowest since the start of census records. This in turn brought about other directions in family life. The smaller number of children makes more care possible for each child. Infants were given much more attention in the twentieth century, on the average, than in preceding centuries. Children are often valued for themselves, rather than as part of a large family work force. Children today are much more apt to be raised by parents and other adults than by siblings.

New Studies of the Family

Ninth, the body of knowledge about children and families increased. Reliable information about how children develop and what their needs are was more widely disseminated. A new discipline, family therapy, emerged. This discipline saw an individual's problems as likely to be symptomatic of an entire family system. Thus treatment was offered for the whole family, not just an "identified patient." The topic of effective communication—within the family and without—was researched and taught. Childhood development, communication, and family therapy are still young and developing disciplines. Nevertheless, they now offer more helpful information and assistance than most families have the time and energy to make use of. Excellent tools for family ministry are emerging.

Increase in Nuclear Families

Tenth, American families have become increasingly mobile. Family historians do not entirely agree that in earlier times there was more emphasis on extended families. However, it cannot be questioned that with many extended families today spread over several states or nations, there must be increasing reliance on the nuclear family. Not only may grandparents and other kinfolk live at a distance, friendships are often disturbed as the nuclear family uproots itself in pursuit of a better job, education, or other opportunity. As one observer noted, America became a nation of strangers (Packard 1972).

Growth of the Mass Media

Eleventh, several new media forms were invented and invaded the home. Radio, television, movies, video and audio cassettes, records, and tapes, as well as books, magazines, and newspapers, exerted powerful influences on families. As media pioneer Marshall McLuhan noted, "The family circle has widened. The whirlpool of information fathered by electronic media . . . far surpasses any possible influence Mom and Dad can now bring to bear. Character is no longer shaped by only two earnest, fumbling experts. Now all the world's a sage" (quoted by Marx and Quesnell 1971, pp. 43–44).

Resulting Changes in Family Styles

Scholars of family life, aware of these influences, debated whether family life would endure beyond the last quarter of the twentieth century. While they were discussing this possibility, families muddled into an amazing variety of family styles. Here are nine notable changes.

1. The "traditional" American family—intact marriage, father employed outside the home, mother not, at least two children—has shrunk to about 10 percent of all families.

2. Persons who marry have a lesser chance that they will stay married till death. The Skolnicks noted that "the freedom of modern family life is bought at the price of fragility and instability in family ties" (1974, p. 12). On the other hand, as some observed, approximately the same percentage of married partners experience premature separation as in earlier centuries. The only difference is that death used to be what separated couples. In the twentieth century, it is more likely to be divorce.

3. An increasing number of persons raise children as single parents.

At the same time, a larger percentage of children live with at least one parent. In earlier times, a single parent was more likely to put children in a home for foundlings, an orphanage, or a foster home. In the twentieth century single parents raise children themselves.

4. Divorced partners are more likely to hear the court assign joint custody of children. This means that two adults who feel they can't live together will still have to meet regularly. They need to make joint decisions about their children and transfer them back and forth between two homes.

5. A large proportion of those who divorce marry new partners and enter into stepfamilies. Frequently such persons leave one difficult family relationship and enter into one even more complex. Two contracting partners might come with children, varying ties to ex-spouses, ex-in-laws, and more. A larger, extremely complex network of persons will need to start all over again to build a family-type community.

6. In the vast majority of couples, both partners are employed. Skills are needed in negotiating the use of those scarcest of family resources, energy and time. Many employment situations (health care, police, fire protection, sales in shopping malls, factory shift work) have invaded family schedules. As a result, there is less time to be together. Persons in career military service have learned to adjust to constant changes in togetherness and separation. Married persons who discover that career opportunities call them to different places become commuter couples.

7. A significant number of people marry partners from other religions, ethnic groups, or nations, thus adding still other dimensions to their marriages. Some who adopt welcome international or special-needs children into their homes.

8. Many couples delay having children, have fewer children, or decide against having any at all. Such couples have begun to redefine marriage without children.

9. Some people elect singleness as a choice. Others, single or married, admit other people's children into their families, permanently or temporarily.

These changes are not passing fads. They are part of the social landscape in the last decade of the twentieth century and beyond.

A Biblical-Theological Perspective

So far we have reported these changes dispassionately and not raised questions of theological and ethical evaluation. We turn now to that task. We need to know how to respond to families in these changing circumstances.

A helpful way to assess the changing nature of American families is with the perspective offered by H. Richard Niebuhr in *Christ and Culture*. He noted that while persons have tried to live out their own lives in commitment to Jesus, they have also engaged the cultures in which they lived. There are at least five different stances Christians have taken in the dialogue between Christ and culture (Niebuhr 1951, pp. 39–44).

1. *Christ against culture*. Christ is seen as opposed to many of culture's norms. Christ confronts persons with the challenge of an either-or decision. One is called to reject what is happening in culture and choose Christ.

2. *Christ of culture*. In this view, Christ is seen as the great hero of human cultural history. His life and teachings are viewed as significant human achievements, his life as the epitome of human values. Jesus is considered as part of culture, the product of a social heritage to be transmitted and conserved.

3. *Christ above culture*. While persons with this viewpoint share some of the viewpoints of the preceding group, they see Christ as also discontinuous with social life and its culture. Christ comes into life from above and beyond, offering gifts that are beyond human aspiration and effort. In this view Christ relates persons to a supernatural society and a new value center not found within culture.

4. *Christ and culture in paradox*. The emphasis here is on the duality and inescapable authority of both Christ and culture. The Christian lives in the tension of being obedient to two authorities that do not agree. In turn, the believer is subject to two moralities, as a citizen of two worlds that are largely opposed to each other. Therefore, life is one of polarity and tension. The follower of Christ lives precariously and sinfully in the hope of a justification that lies beyond history.

5. *Christ the transformer of culture*. Persons with this viewpoint concur with the first and fourth group. Human nature is fallen, and this perversion is seen in culture and transmitted by it. However, Christ is the converter, the transformer of humans and hence of culture. The person who is converted is converted in society and in turn is part of the transformation of society.

Of those five stances (each of which has been chosen at times by devout Christians), which is most appropriate when thinking about contemporary family issues?

We are sympathetic to each of these perspectives. Yet it seems to us that the stance most faithful to the New Testament is the fifth one, Christ the transformer of culture. Admittedly, it will not be possible to live totally consistently with this stance. In all of life, certain stubborn, persistent realities must be dealt with as they are. And yet the vision, the dream, the goal will always be of Christ as the transformer. This transformation will be of individuals, marriages, and families and of society.

With this motif of Christ as transformer, we seek a biblical hermeneutic that will be harmonious and coherent with our perspective. Our assumptions about biblical interpretation include the following:

1. The Bible holds basic authority for us. It is a dynamic authority. We find truth in the statements that the Bible *is* the word of God, *contains* the word of God, and *becomes* the word of God.

2. The Holy Spirit was active in the writing of the Bible and is active in the reading, exploring, and interpreting of the Bible.

3. The Bible is a community document created by the church and to be interpreted in community and dialogue with others who are also exploring.

4. Each believer is invested with "soul freedom." In regard to Bible study this means that each believer, endowed with salvation and with the Holy Spirit, can responsibly engage in biblical interpretation. Part of the responsibility of this gift is to be in dialogue with careful biblical scholars and with other persons of faith.

After beginning with those four basic affirmations there are four issues related to the concerns we raise in this book.

5. It is a creative engagement of scripture to put to it the questions raised by a different culture and a new age. As students of the changing family and of scriptures, we find ourselves raising questions of faith and ethics that we have never asked before. While this engagement of scripture is often an uncomfortable exercise, it is also exciting and contains the possibility of being a fruitful venture.

6. In raising such questions we become aware of a mix of at least two types of material in the Bible. There are culturally conditioned perspectives, for the Bible was written in an amazing diversity of cultures. There are also normative teachings. This leads to a delicate task. As Virginia Ramey Mollenkott has put it, "One cannot absolutize the culture in which the Bible was written." In reading one should discern carefully between cultural assumptions and explicit biblical teaching. In Mollenkott's words, we need to distinguish between what is written "for an age" and what is written for all times (1977, p. 91).

7. We discover that there is development, growth, and transformation from one passage to another. There is a trajectory of growing revelation, insight, and obedience. For example, the teachings about marriage and family in Ephesians 5 and 6 (given the cultural setting in which they were written) represent a daring transformation of then-existing practices. Perhaps the way to be faithful to such a statement is to carry it the next steps farther in our culture. We may be called to be Christian revolutionaries, used of God in transforming contemporary

families! Old Testament professor Harrell Beck used to say there was only one thing wrong with the Bible—it has a back cover on it! Perhaps by discovering the transforming principles and carrying on where scriptural trajectories lead, we can live with a Bible that doesn't have a back cover on it. The story will continue.

8. This leads us to one more item in our hermeneutic. We will not be surprised if we encounter dissonance and conflict in such Bible study. We will not run away from these conflicts but will try to stay with them. Perhaps the conflict will be between a biblical writer and his audience. It may be between various biblical passages. The dissonance might occur between theology taught in the Bible and practices described in the Bible (in which case we think that obedience to what is implied by the theology should take precedence). The struggle can arise between what one feels out of Christian compassion and what one seems to find in scripture. We believe that such conflicts can be revelatory. It is when we struggle over such issues with vulnerability, and with openness to the leading of the Holy Spirit, that light comes, transformation occurs, and there is new insight and direction.

We are lovers of Bible, of church, and of contemporary changing families. It is our hope to bring these three into closer dialogue. To do this, we risk interpreting the Bible in relation to these matters. In so doing we do not confuse our interpretation with scripture itself. Rather, we are two Christians trying to look with new eyes both at the Bible and at a contemporary issue crying out for Christian analysis, compassion, and action.

The approach we have described has much in common with the following section of a recent declaration of faith (PCUS 1976, p. 161):

Relying on the Holy Spirit,
    who opens our eyes and hearts,
    we affirm our freedom to interpret Scripture responsibly.
God has chosen to address [God's] inspired Word to us
    through diverse and varied human writings.
Therefore we use the best available methods
    to understand them in their historical and cultural settings
    and the literary forms in which they are cast.
When we encounter apparent tensions and conflicts
    in what Scripture teaches us to believe and do,
    the final appeal must be to the authority of Christ.
Acknowledging that authority,
    comparing Scripture with Scripture,
    listening with respect to fellow-believers past and present,
        we anticipate that the Holy Spirit
        will enable us to interpret faithfully
        God's Word for our time and place.

Here then are the basic biblical principles that inform our theology of ministry with the changing family. Others that apply to particular family styles will be offered in subsequent chapters.

The Importance and Power of Marriage and Family Relationships

The Bible affirms the importance and power of the human relationship. In particular, it emphasizes the significance of marriage and of the family.

God has entrusted tremendous power to the human relationship. It is there that a person finds revealed one's identity, power, esteem, faith, worth, place in history, and future. Through the human relationship one is comforted in sorrow, sustained in despair, encouraged in failure or defeat, and doubly enriched in sharing victories and triumphs. The human relationship is God's means of helping persons realize the existence and presence of a God of love and forgiveness. Most persons decide to be followers of God in response to an invitation from someone whose relationship they treasure. However, relationships have equal power to hurt and destroy. Relationships can cause grief or despair, and can lead one to question one's own self-worth or significance.

Marriage is uniquely endowed with all the relational power that we have described, and this is part of God's plan for it. In Genesis 1, God creates male and female and tells them to be fruitful and multiply. In Genesis 2, the man rejoices in the woman and calls her "bone of my bones and flesh of my flesh." The story goes on to speak of the primacy of the marriage relationship: "a man leaves his father and his mother and cleaves to his wife, and they become one flesh." At that point they exist in innocent celebration of each other: "And the man and his wife were both naked, and were not ashamed" (Gen. 2:23–25). Jesus spoke of these passages in Mark 10:2–12. He affirmed that in the light of God's intent, marriage is a significant institution which must never be taken lightly (Efird 1985, pp. 54–55).

In order to assure that marriage and family will fulfill God's intention, these relationships are covenantal—they are based on vows, open to renegotiation, concerned with life-and-death issues, and subject to various internal and external sanctions (Brueggemann 1977, p. 18).

In addition to marriage, the relationship of family holds a vital significance in biblical teaching. Walter Brueggemann notes that in the biblical faith *"the family is the primary unit of meaning which shapes and defines reality. . . .* It is the family that provides deep secure roots into the past, holds visions for the future, a sense of purpose and a set of priorities for the present" (ibid.).

In Bible teachings, the family provided many functions for its children. The family gave children names and in so doing expressed anticipation of the destiny for each new member. The family nurtured children through storytelling, instruction, guidance, and discipline. The family helped the child remember the past of the family and of the nation, a holy history. The family provided the means for its members to honor each other. The family managed the family estate or inheritance and saw that it was properly passed on from generation to generation. This was true whether such inheritance was tangible or largely symbolic. Family identity was preserved and communicated. The family also helped make hope possible in children by pointing to promises and potential that were yet to be claimed (Brueggemann 1977, p. 22).

Clearly the Bible ascribes great worth, significance, and power to those relationships called marriage and family. Persons are entrusted with their marriages and families by God and are accountable for making these relationships achieve their intended purpose. Society is likewise held accountable by God for the quality of justice that undergirds these relationships.

Support for Those Whose Marriages and Families Disintegrate

Our next biblical perspective is difficult but crucial. The Bible challenges those who would dissolve marriage and family covenants too readily. At the same time, it recognizes that this disruption, though tragic, does sometimes occur. When this happens, the biblical perspective encourages us to offer support, forgiveness, and help to the end that persons may be healed. There is the further hope that those involved will be empowered for whatever family life remains or whatever family life will evolve for them.

In light of Jesus' direct statements on divorce, this perspective may be open to question. There are a number of biblical teachings and considerations, however, that lead us in this direction.

There is in the Bible the acknowledgment that divorce does occur. As a matter of fact, it is discussed in the Old Testament in a variety of ways. This seems to indicate that divorce must have been a relatively frequent event. When, in Matthew 5:32, Jesus challenged a too-permissive granting of divorces, he mentioned one condition in which one might be granted. That exception clause is usually translated "except for adultery" or "except on the ground of unchastity." James Efird points out that the word thus translated is the Greek term *porneia*, which actually has a wide range of meanings. For example, it is used to refer to incestuous relationships, illicit marriages, cultic prostitution, disloyalty in a general sense, greedy love of money, pride, injustice, evil, and unworthy worship practices. He concludes, "To limit the meaning of the word strictly to sexual immorality of some sort may be far too rigid an interpretation and may well limit the original meaning of the saying" (1985, pp. 57–58). We follow Efird's lead here. With him we recognize that there are behaviors that are destructive to marriage. If earnest effort to change these behaviors proves fruitless, termination of the marriage is understandable and justifiable.

As we put together the strands of Jesus' teaching on such themes, we are helped by Myrna and Robert Kysar's summary. They note that Jesus' teaching contains two points of focus. On the one hand there is "the absolute will of God, or the creative intent of God." When Jesus proclaims God's absolute will, he is offering an ethic for disciples who commit to the kingdom of God here and now. Jesus is not producing a new law, subject to legalistic judgments and demands. Rather, he is describing radical discipleship obedience lived as a foretaste of the kingdom of God. His teachings about divorce in the gospels are part of that aspect—the absolute will or creative intent of God.

On the other hand, Jesus proclaims "the absolute love of God, or the redemptive intent of God" (Kysar and Kysar 1978, p. 54). In this aspect of his teaching, he speaks of a God who creates institutions (such as Sabbath) for human beings, not vice versa. When Jesus proclaims God's love for God's little and weak ones, when he parties with the outcast of that society, when he freely forgives, he is expressing a lavish divine love. The implications of that love have only begun to be spelled out in the pages of the New Testament. These implications are not given in any detail. For example, how might Jesus have responded to persons whose marriage had failed? There may be a few clues in his accepting-confronting style with the woman of Samaria in John 4. The Christian leader will want to explore those implications, to ask, How does a loving, gracious God respond to these changing families? And therefore how should I?

It is a clear biblical teaching that God wills the salvation of individuals and of institutions (such as marriage and family). One translation of the word "salvation" means "health, wholeness, healing, wholesomeness." Whole, healthy persons in whole, healthy relationships—that certainly is God's will for marriage and family. When that is lacking, it is right to try to heal the marriage. However, if such efforts fail, it is appropriate and fitting to end a destructive relationship. Robert Sinks has written, "Whenever marriage serves to crush what is genuinely human, then it must yield to the higher principle of the Great Commandment" (1977, p. 379).

These are difficult matters about which to write. We find ourselves in one of Niebuhr's "Christ and culture in paradox" situations. On the one hand, we reject any notions of marriage as a convenient and casual relationship. We refuse to think of marriage as merely a two-party relationship for fun and fulfillment, with divorce on demand. On the other hand, we repent of narrow Christian judgmentalism that lays heavy burdens of guilt on persons who find it wisest to terminate a marriage. We are sad that some churches do not offer support, care, and aid to divorcing, single, and remarried persons.

Our biblical perspective leads us to a middle ground. Christian churches should do everything they can to hold high the covenant of marriage and family and to equip people to marry healthily and permanently. At the same time, the church should be ready to offer care when married folk experience crisis, either in terminating a marriage or in struggling to build a good new one.

Biblical Support for Diversity of Families

The Bible contains no single definition of family. Rather, the term is used to describe a variety of configurations. These include both persons who have some kinship ties and persons who do not. Sometimes the term "family" includes the entire household—male servant, female servant, sojourner in the gate, the Levite, the fatherless, and the widow (Ex. 20:10; Deut. 24:20). The variety of family types that occur within the biblical material is wide and fascinating.

As a matter of fact, in Jesus' own experience there was quite a diversity of family styles. There was an unmarried pregnant teenager, with threats of "divorce" of the betrothal, in Matthew 1:19; a transient couple; a refugee family; a nuclear family, about which the only recorded story is of family conflict with an adolescent in Luke 2:41–50; probably a single-parent family—Joseph never appears again after Luke 2; life as an unmarried single; and group life that might be termed "intentional family," consisting of those men and women who banded together in support of Jesus and his ministry (Teague 1988, pp. 29–31).

The clear implication here is that we can have equal freedom in describing membership of families and in addressing family styles as they emerge.

Our Continually Creating and Redeeming God and the Family

The Bible portrays a God who is continually creating and redeeming, who constantly surprises us by doing new things and resurrecting new life and power into the world. Therefore, change may be a sign of God's creative presence. Adjusting to change may well be a creative response.

Christians believe that the future toward which God is calling them is always new. It may well be that these insights apply to the family. Pastoral theologian Herbert Anderson writes (1984, pp. 31–32), "God is not finished with the family. As an institution it continues to participate in the changing character of all reality. . . . The future of the family is thus open, not just in response to the diversity of needs but because God is acting to make something new."

The many family styles that are emerging may be but a sign of the extravagance of this continually creating and redeeming God. Again, Anderson suggests (p. 78), "Families, like people, fish, flowers, and snowflakes, are wonderfully and frightfully different. Where the family is concerned, there is no one design that has divine approval." In the chapters that follow we will describe an amazing number of family styles that are evolving in our society, yet we only scratch the surface of this diversity. The variety of ways that families work together, play together, enforce discipline, offer upbuilding and support, and claim their family history defies classification.

Not all family styles arise out of happiness. Some come out of suffering, grief, alienation, abandonment, tragedy. It is at this point that God's most powerful act of surprise and redemption applies. God raised Jesus from the dead. Our God is a God of resurrection, of rebirth and new beginnings. When families (and individual members) are not crushed by tragedy but find new ways to create strong healthy relationships, that is a sign that the God of resurrection is still at work! (Kysar and Kysar 1978, p. 104). We hold to the conviction that the work of our creating, redeeming, resurrecting God may be seen in changing families.

The Family in Its Larger Context

The Bible never speaks of the family in isolation. The family exists in a larger context. In the Old Testament that context is Israel, as extended family, family of families, people of God, one's nation. In the New Testament, the family's context is the church, the new Israel, one's household of faith.

That famous passage, the Shema, in which parents are instructed to pass God's teaching and guidance to their children, is addressed to the community: "Hear, O Israel: The LORD our God is one LORD; . . . and you shall teach [these words] diligently to your children, and shall talk of them when you sit in your house, and when you walk by the way, and when you lie down, and when you rise" (Deut. 6:4, 7–9).

Faithfulness to this insight requires that the church be a true family of families of all types, an extended family. It also encourages awareness as to whether society is enhancing or inhibiting family welfare, as individual families live in that wider context. Wallace C. Smith has demonstrated how the black church has functioned in this way for three centuries, enabling black people to survive slavery and racist oppression. Recovery of this historical model is critical to meeting the risks many black families face today. It may also point the way for the whole church toward a renewed family ministry (Smith 1985).

The Family as Means, Not End

The God of the Bible calls persons to accountability for all idolatries in which they might engage. One of the subtle idolatries in which people engage is that of family. When family is seen as end in itself, it has become an idol, a god.

The Bible makes clear that, as important as family is, it is not an end in itself. Jesus came and spoke of the kingdom of God that takes primacy over family claims (Mark 3:20–35). The gospel calls for a radical loyalty that transcends the bonds of family (Anderson 1984, p. 16).

In the Bible there is often a tension between the natural family and the family of faith. Abraham is called to leave his family and go to a new place in obedience to God. Jesus warns that a result of obedience to him may be to "set a man against his father, and a daughter against her mother. . . . He who loves father or mother . . . [or] son or daughter more than me is not worthy of me" (Matt. 10:35–37). Again, Jesus asks, "Who are my mother and my brothers?" He responds in Mark 3:33–35 that they are whoever does the will of God (Brueggemann 1977, pp. 22–23).

Every family needs to ask hard questions: In what way is our family enhancing each member's participation in the larger family of faith? In service to the world? How are we inhibiting our family members in these regards? What is our covenant with one another and with God? A basic task of Christian leaders is to help those served see family as means, not end.

The Biblical View of the Purpose for Family Ministry

Our discoveries lead us to a basic conclusion: The Bible mandates empowering families so that they meet basic human needs and equip their members in turn to be agents of God's redemptive power.

From such a biblical-theological perspective we now undertake a direct examination of family dynamics and needs and of the opportunities for ministry with some of the emerging family styles we have mentioned.

Resources and References

Anderson, Herbert. 1984. *The Family and Pastoral Care.* Philadelphia: Fortress Press.

Bane, Mary Jo. 1976. *Here to Stay: American Families in the Twentieth Century.* New York: Basic Books.

Barbeau, Clayton C., ed. 1971. *Future of the Family.* New York: Bruce Publishing Co.

Berger, Briggite, and Peter L. Berger. 1983. *The War Over the Family:*

Capturing the Middle Ground. Garden City, N.Y.: Doubleday & Co., Anchor Books.

Bronfenbrenner, Urie. 1979. *The Ecology of Human Development: Experiments by Nature and Design.* Cambridge, Mass.: Harvard University Press.

Brueggemann, Walter. 1977. "The Covenanted Family: A Zone for Humanness." *Journal of Current Social Issues,* vol. 14, no. 1 (Winter 1977), pp. 17–23.

Casler, Lawrence. 1974. *Is Marriage Necessary?* New York: Human Sciences Press.

Cooper, David. 1970. *The Death of the Family.* New York: Pantheon Books.

Efird, James M. 1985. *Marriage and Divorce: What the Bible Says.* Nashville: Abingdon Press.

Greeley, Andrew, ed. 1979. *The Family in Crisis or in Transition: A Sociological and Theological Perspective.* New York: Seabury Press.

Kysar, Myrna, and Robert Kysar. 1978. *The Asundered: Biblical Teachings on Divorce and Remarriage.* Atlanta: John Knox Press.

Marx, Paul, and Jack Quesnell. 1971. "Family Life: The Agony and the Ecstasy." In Clayton C. Barbeau, ed., *Future of the Family.* New York: Bruce Publishing Co.

Mollenkott, Virginia Ramey. 1977. *Women, Men, and the Bible.* Nashville: Abingdon Press.

Niebuhr, H. Richard. 1951. *Christ and Culture.* New York: Harper & Brothers.

Packard, Vance. 1972. *A Nation of Strangers.* New York: David McKay Co.

PCUS. 1976. *The Proposed Book of Confessions.* Atlanta: Presbyterian Church in the United States.

Ruether, Rosemary. 1984. "Feminism, Church and Family in the 1980s." *American Baptist Quarterly,* vol. 13 (March), pp. 21–30.

Scanzoni, Letha Dawson, and John Scanzoni. 1981. *Men, Women, and Change: A Sociology of Marriage and Family,* 2nd ed. New York: McGraw-Hill Book Co.

Shorter, Edward. 1975. *The Making of the Modern Family.* New York: Basic Books.

Sinks, Robert F. 1977. "A Theology of Divorce." *Christian Century,* April 20, pp. 376–379.

Skolnick, Arlene, and Jerome H. Skolnick. 1974. *Intimacy, Family, and Society.* Boston: Little, Brown and Co.

Smith, Wallace Charles. 1985. *The Church in the Life of the Black Family.* Valley Forge, Pa.: Judson Press.

Spong, John Shelby. 1984. "Can the Church Bless Divorce?" *Christian Century,* November 28, pp. 1126–1127.

Stearns, Peter N. 1979. *Be a Man!* New York: Homes and Meier Publishers.

Sullivan, Teresa. 1979. "Longer Lives and Life-long Relations: A Life Table Exegesis." In Andrew Greeley, ed., *The Family in Crisis or in Transition.* New York: Seabury Press.

Teague, Willie S. 1988. "What Is a Christian Family?" *Weavings,* vol. 3, no. 1 (January/February), pp. 26–31.

U.S. Bureau of the Census. 1975. *Historical Statistics of the United States, Colonial Times to 1970.* Washington, D.C.: U.S. Government Printing Office.

2

The Effect of Changing Employment Patterns

Throughout history, employment has had an impact on the family. The nature, demands, rewards, and location of people's work has tremendously influenced family living.

In the era of farmers and artisans pursuing their trades at home or nearby, husband and wife were involved in many activities together. They shared the work that earned the family's livelihood and the responsibility (including care, education, and job training) for their children. Some of the children entered these enterprises with their parents.

The Industrial Revolution brought many changes. For one thing, it separated workplace from home. For a time, father, mother, and children all worked at the factories. Machines controlled people, a dehumanizing change. Gradually child labor laws protected the children from this exploitative labor. The rise of the labor movement forced other changes that made the workplace safer and more humane for adults.

For the more affluent, the expectation developed that the father would go to a place removed from his home. There he would perform the work that would provide income for the family. The mother would remain at home and perform the household tasks and child care functions. Children in such a family needed to know more things than their parents could teach them, so a larger part of the children's education was provided outside the home.

Many families could not afford the luxury of this arrangement. Among these were marginally employed persons, new immigrants, and persons who suffered discrimination in job opportunities and pay. All of these needed income from the labor of each able-bodied member of the household.

Still, one family employment pattern (father gone, mother home) came to be identified as the ideal. Some writers of child-rearing literature assumed it to be the only way for a family to be healthy.

Then, in the twentieth century, things began to change. In the 1920s an increasing number of women entered the work force. Again in World War II many women filled places in the work force formerly occupied by men who had joined the armed forces. For large numbers of these women, the presumption was probably that one would work for the duration of the war, until marriage, or until the birth of children.

In the latter half of the twentieth century, patterns changed even more, and rapidly. Of mothers with children between 6 and 17, the percentage participating in the labor force outside the home was

39.0 in 1960
49.2 in 1970
61.7 in 1980
70.6 in 1987

This growth included mothers with small children as well. In 1960, 19 percent of mothers with children under 6 years of age were employed outside their homes. By 1970 that figure had grown to 30 percent. It was 45 percent by 1980 and 57 percent by 1987 (U.S. Bureau of the Census 1988, p. 374). At least 62 percent of all married couples today have two wage earners (Stuart and Jacobson 1985, p. 141).

Two things have changed in the late twentieth century: (1) Women are more likely to be working throughout their lifetimes, including the infancy and childhood of their offspring; (2) women are entering a wide range of careers that demand as great a work investment as men give. Both the length of employment for many women and their range of working opportunities has increased.

While the trend shown by this information is obvious, what is not so clear is what this change means to the family members themselves. We shall probe this by looking more directly at some of the emerging family styles.

The Two-Career Couple

Let's visualize a two-career family. Jeff and Judy are in their mid-thirties. Both are committed to their careers and to their family. They have three children, ages 12, 9, and 4.While at least keeping this effort alive, they daily have many questions. Here are a baker's dozen that Jeff and Judy ask.

1. "Whose job has priority?" In selecting jobs, do we assume that the husband's career is given higher consideration? Or should we take turns in having the decision-making power about moves that might contribute to career advancement? What if one of our jobs progresses better than the other? What if one of our jobs doesn't move at all, or moves with great difficulty?

2. "Why isn't dinner ready?" Whose work is the household work? If a wife works outside the home, is she expected to do all the traditionally assigned roles as well? Jeff and Judy readily agreed with what the Halls, another two-career couple, wrote: "Most fights over women's rights take place in the kitchen, not in the state capital" (Hall and Hall 1979, p. 113).

Some studies show that the woman decreases the hours she devotes to homemaking and parental tasks when she enters the labor force. But this research indicates that the husband and children do not substantially increase theirs. On the other hand, there are studies that say that children of working mothers develop more initiative, responsibility, and care-giving abilities.

Judy and Jeff use a shared-duty system. They are attempting to make it flexible in regard to each other's work schedules, capabilities, rushed times, and so on. Still, there is an uneasy feeling of breaking with the way their parents had divided work.

3. "Why can't we get it done tonight?" The overscheduled couple feels like a juggler trying to keep too many balls in the air at the same time. Fatigue is a constant problem. Jeff and Judy have discovered that the issue is deciding what is really essential and what is luxury in their self-expectations. In time, they have found that they can modify habits and routines. They can also reduce some of their self-imposed requirements about house, lawn, and car, and can consider moving into a condo where there is less responsibility. While Jeff and Judy decrease their tensions over this issue, it never entirely disappears.

4. "Why aren't we having any fun?" The answer, they discover, is that they are both workaholics. They have little time for play, for each other, or for spiritual replenishment. People can live on their heritage and their stored resources for a while. The time comes, however, when they need renewal, relaxation, and refreshment. Provision for personal and couple refreshment is basic for survival.

5. "What ever happened to . . . ?" Judy and Jeff sometimes feel a sense of isolation from friends and acquaintances. Their already crowded schedules prohibit their planning leisurely dinner parties or other time-consuming entertaining of friends. "How do we make time

for old friends? How do they make time for us?" These issues are basic to the well-being of two-career couples.

6. "Whose children are these and who is responsible for their care?" There is need for child care when they are absent from their children and for quality time with them. Experiences shared by many employed couples reveal that their plans include everything but a sick or injured child. That one additional strain on time often feels like more than a couple can endure (Rowatt and Rowatt 1980, pp. 16–19).

7. Jeff and Judy occasionally have to ask, "Is there any competition between us regarding our careers? And, if so, how do we handle it? Is it OK for Judy to acquire a more advanced degree than Jeff holds? Does it matter who gets the better pay, more recognition, the faster promotions and raises? And even if we escape competition within our relationship, do others impose it from without?"

8. "What about money?" Couples with two paychecks face some new issues on money management and influence. Power structures change when wives become "breadwinners" also. Some issues that were clear now have to be renegotiated. What do we do with two paychecks? Of the money I earn, how much is ours and how much is mine? What if we have different expectations about whether extra money should be saved or used for present enjoyment? What about giving to church and charity? (Do we need to give more since we have less time to offer?) What about socially aware investment? Where do we put the money (in whose account), and who keeps our financial records? Couples who are relaxed about finances and have similar values about money may find this easy. Many couples will not. Frank, open discussion and decision-making is needed lest an asset become a liability.

9. "How do we juggle vacations?" Some years, Jeff and Judy have difficulty coordinating these important times. Their careers are in different fields. They envy their friends who have an easier time of it. Two workers at the same plant, or two educators, or two ministers can often manage their vacation breaks together. If a couple cannot always plan to take vacations together, do they have a mutual understanding of what are fitting vacations if they must be taken apart?

10. "I still want to . . . When can we . . . ?" There is the matter of romance and sexuality. Too often, pressure, tension, and busyness crowd out time to keep alive or renew a sense of loving, romantic fellowship. Judy and Jeff ponder what one no-nonsense sex therapist advised in an article: Two-career couples should schedule time for romance and sexuality as they schedule everything else. Or else, he said, it just probably won't happen.

11. "What about opposite-sex friendships among one's peers at work?" Jeff and Judy are aware that work is where one puts in the most

hours and puts on one's best appearance. Furthermore, work is where the persons are who share one's triumphs most intimately and give support in frustration or disappointment. This often leads to a sense of closeness to coworkers. Judy and Jeff feel the need to discuss opposite-sex friends and colleagues at work. Can one socialize with them? In groups only? One on one? Is some affectionate exchange acceptable or not? The awareness of being special or attractive to a coworker is a rewarding experience, one that enhances a feeling of self-worth. This can be threatening, though, to a marriage that they both want to keep good and strong. How do partners handle this in such a way that their own integrity as a couple is maintained?

12. "Where is the support? Why are there so many barriers?" Jeff and Judy felt a tremendous sense of insight when they read a discussion of this matter by Lynda L. Holmstrom (1972, pp. 1–2). She notes that our society has not yet become sensitive to the needs of two-career couples.

> These [two career] couples are "bucking the system," and they have had to face a whole series of barriers which assume that only one spouse will work and that, furthermore, it is the husband who will do so.
> Many of the barriers encountered by these people fall into three main categories—the rigid structure of the professions, the isolation of the small, modern family, and the current equation of masculinity with superiority. They include such things as the definition of career as requiring single-minded devotion to work, frequent pressures to move geographically for career advancement, the expectation that some jobs will be held by men while their wives devote time and energy to ancillary activities such as entertaining, and the difficulty of raising children when both spouses work. Although these barriers may be altered or removed in the future, at present they constitute severe obstacles for the two career family.

These obstacles do exist. It may be that the two-career couple will encounter critical attitudes. They may experience inflexibility, such as parent-teacher conferences scheduled only during the workday. There may be a lack of adequate services such as child care. Society may offer little to help them achieve their twin objectives of career and family.

13. "Should we . . . ?" There are deeper questions about children than we have yet discussed. Jeff and Judy assumed they would have children and that these children could be cared for within their two-career lives. They find, however, that many have held these assumptions up to question.

One question is, Should the two-career couple have children at all? Do they have the time, energy, and other resources to bear and raise children?

Another question is, Can people who have careers be good parents to their children? If so, does this mean long periods when at least one parent should be home? Should one parent be home from the birth of the first child until the last one is in full day school? If not, are children deeply troubled, more maladjusted than other people's children? For a long time, most pediatric literature has seemed to assume so.

Jean Curtis interviewed many working parents in preparation for her book *Working Mothers*. She advises any mother who chooses employment to avoid reading conventional pediatric books. Most of these books assume that children need one constant adult and that this adult must be the mother. She began her study not knowing what to believe about the impact of working mothers on children. Curtis concluded (1976, p. 57) that for many children of working mothers, the impact of the mother's working is positive. Her interviews led her to believe that

• When the parents are employed during the child's early infancy, the child adapts to being cared for by several adults, usually rather easily.

• Contrary to some parents' fears, the child does not forget who the parents are.

• Employed parents often give their children as much attentive care as persons who are with their children all day long.

Curtis quotes a study of children of working parents:

Such children show as much attachment to their mothers as children of mothers who are housewives. This is mainly because the mother who goes off to work every day is likely to realize that her children definitely need a period of playing with her and being with her when she gets home, and she allows for this. In fact, the child may get even more out of the working mom than out of the housewife mom, who may not really feel the need to interact as positively with her child. After all, she may feel, she is always at home anyway.

Up to this point we have spoken of Jeff and Judy. We have located in their story many of the common themes for two-career couples. The Jeffs and Judys are already the majority of American couples. Quite probably their numbers will grow—in spite of these thirteen questions and possibly others as well.

We will leave this couple now. To fill in the picture, we note there is also wide variety among two-career couples.

First, there are differences in attitudes about employment. For example, Stuart and Jacobson make a distinction between a career and a job. In their description, a career is "the pursuit of work as an end in itself." Because the work offers many intrinsic rewards, careerists may devote much time and energy to it. On the other hand, a job "is essentially either a way of earning money or of just getting out of the house" (1985, p. 145). The job is seen as less rewarding than spending time with family and friends. Whether each partner regards his or her own and the other's employment as job or career has an impact on their two-employment experience.

Second, there is variation in how persons feel about the desirability of dual employment. Caroline Bird has noted at least four different responses: (1) reluctant working wives—both partners prefer that the wife not work outside the home but necessity dictates otherwise; (2) submissive working wives—women who would prefer to specialize in homemaking but whose husbands want them to work outside the home; (3) defiant housewives—women who choose to be employed although their husbands do not like it and resist (this group includes at least one in five working wives from Bird's research); (4) contemporary working wives—women who are working because that is what both they and their husbands want (1979, pp. 30–40).

Third, there is diversity in the ways couples adapt to dual employment. Francine and Douglas Hall suggest there are basically two responses a couple can make. One is a traditional response—to assume that although the wife is employed, the sex-role expectations about all household, family, and parental duties remain the same. They call an alternative response the "protean" style. This term comes from the Greek god of the sea, Proteus, who was able to change his shape spontaneously—from animal, to water, to rock—as frequently as he chose. It was his adaptability that guaranteed his survival. The Halls suggest such a marriage/family style can be chosen. Like Proteus, both partners develop the flexibility so necessary in a marriage with changing employment patterns. As the Halls play with this image, they see four subtypes among the couples they studied:

1. Accommodators. Usually one partner is high in career involvement and low in home involvement; the other is just the opposite. Since each may be able to order priorities clearly, they can work out the shared work issues and achieve personal satisfaction with each other.

2. Adversaries. Both partners are highly involved in their careers and have a very small investment in home, family, and partner support. Both want a well-ordered home and well-raised children. Neither wants to invest time and effort in this, however. Such couples experience much stress as they compete with each other over priorities and obligations.

3. Allies. Either both partners are highly involved in their careers, or both are highly committed to their home roles. As with the accommodators, their priorities are clearly defined. They will make whatever adjustments are needed to make it possible for both to be accommodated in their individual and couple priorities.

4. Acrobats. These are marriages where both partners are highly involved in each of their roles. "They can be thought of as rather frantic acrobats" (Hall and Hall 1979, p. 25). Such persons give equal value to home and career roles. They experience as much conflict over these matters as do the adversaries. Unlike the adversaries, however, their conflicts are internal, not with each other. They simply want to do it all well.

The Halls conclude, "The two-career couple is . . . intimately bound up in social changes toward greater freedom, equality, and self-fulfillment. . . . The dilemma is how to combine individual fulfillment and freedom with responsibility to one's mate" (1979, p. 26).

With all these variations, two-career families live with some issues that their grandparents never faced. Their challenges of family living also differ markedly from the one-career couples in their community.

The Couple with a Househusband

A couple may conclude that one of them should specialize in employment and the other in home and child care. It would seem logical that either spouse could choose either role—except for long-held sex-role stereotypes. However, increasing numbers of couples are breaking out of these stereotypes. Some discover that the role strain is fairly minor, less than anticipated.

There are now numbers of men who may be considered "househusbands" in the same way that some women may be considered "housewives." How many househusbands are there? In 1950, the number of men reported by the census as outside the labor force because they were "keeping house" was 81,000. By 1971, the number reported was 296,000, an increase of 265 percent. However, William Beer, who carried on a study of househusbands, would suggest a different definition (1983, p. 10). He contends that a man is a househusband if he does 50 percent or more of the household tasks and child care, whether he has some employment outside the home or not. He interviewed those who were househusbands by this definition.

Why do men do housework? The answers given were varied. Some were unemployed (by choice or circumstance) and so undertook housework as a means of contributing something to the household. Others did so out of a sense of fairness since the wife was employed also. Some followed role models of fathers or other men. Others took over tasks by choice and gained a real sense of pride and craftsmanship from it.

He asked, "Do househusbands like housework?" Beer discovered that there was about the same range of love-hate responses to housework among men as among women. He quoted a published memoir,

Mike McGrady's *The Kitchen Sink Papers: My Life as a Househus-band*. In this book, McGrady reports on a year in which he switched roles with his wife. Beer felt that the ambivalence McGrady described was quite typical for the men he interviewed. Wrote McGrady (1975, pp. 177–178):

> The year . . . had been boring, repetitive, dreary and at times just plain dumb—yet, I had enjoyed it more than any year in recent memory. At least I had been aware of it. In living a life of deadlines, a life where one assignment overlaps another, time vanishes. This year I took walks and noted season changes and enjoyed sunsets. This year I became a real part of the family, maybe for the first time.

One househusband spoke of enjoying the freedom and the crea-tivity he could express. His time at home had included many home-improvement and decoration projects as well as cooking and cleaning. His greatest fear was becoming obsolete—losing ground in a rapidly changing profession. He also worried about the gap of time on his resume.

How does housework change men? Beer discovered that the expe-rience of being extensively involved in housework did have an impact on the men. He suggested, "Housework changes men's feelings: about themselves, about their spouses, and about work." Negative feelings included an occasional sense of loss of status, tension with one's spouse about priorities, and ambivalence about one's changing role. He discovered, however, that positive reactions outnumbered the negative ones. These men felt greater insight into the problems faced by housewives, more involvement with their children, and improve-ments of their marital relationship. If the man also worked outside the home, he quit identifying himself exclusively in terms of that occupa-tion. Rather he defined himself more in terms of his home relation-ships and nonprofessional work (Beer 1983, p. 89).

Beer suggested that all these changes point to an even more basic influence of househusbanding on men—an overcoming of alienation. Alienation may be seen as a person's separation from one's fellows and from society at large. This is due to the extensive division of labor, the impersonality of bureaucracy, and the vague character of so much work. Seldom do we feel a close connection between ourselves and what we create. He noted, "Housework, by the testimony of some of the men at least, offers an antidote to alienation" (p. 67). He suggests that alienation is overcome through carrying out all phases of a task at home. In addition, work and home become integrated. A person does not work only for abstract values or wages, but rather one works for loved ones. In this, some men experienced a basic therapeutic value in the housework they did.

William Beer concluded his fascinating and positive study of house-husbanding in this manner: "Men and women need each other, particularly in family life, with its myriad kinds of interdependence. Instead of increasing the estrangement . . . the growing numbers of house-husbands foreshadow growing cooperation between the sexes in the family, the most fundamental of human institutions" (p. 118).

Another aspect of househusbanding is the impact that it has on the relationship between fathers and children. Many fathers speak of this as being one of the most rewarding aspects. One study shows that it is equally enriching for the children. Kyle Pruett, a child psychologist at Yale, tested a group of seventeen infants whose fathers stayed home. Pruett discovered that the children were developing at an amazing rate. The youngest group of infants (aged 2 to 12 months) performed problem-solving tasks on the level of babies six to twelve months older than they. Their social skills were two to ten months ahead of schedule. This was true for the older babies (12 to 22 months) as well. Pruett suggested that what distinguished these babies is the amount of love and attention they received from both parents. While the fathers and babies had formed deep attachments to each other, the mothers had developed close attachments to the infants too. Pruett reported, "Most of the mothers breast-fed their babies, often at great inconvenience to themselves." He concluded that these babies are flourishing "because instead of having one and a quarter or one and a half parents, they have two real parents." Two years later, although some of the fathers have returned to work, the babies' rate of development has not slowed (Carro 1983, p. 71).

Another househusband reported that the relationship to his elementary school children and their friends was the most rewarding part for him. He had volunteered to be a "room mother" for one of his children's home room at school. Because of his good discipline skills and his great enjoyment of activities, he was a welcome chaperon on field trips.

Other Employment Patterns for Couples

Some couples have discovered that their choice may not be the one- or two-career marriage. Perhaps it lies somewhere in the middle. Possibly, either out of choice or from economic necessity, they desire to have a one-and-a-quarter- or one-and-a-half-paycheck marriage. There are at least two ways this can be accomplished.

One is the career/earner model. In this case, only one partner has the kind of career that demands a major commitment of time and energy. The other partner also works some—perhaps part time, perhaps nearly full time—outside the home. This partner places an equal or higher priority on home, family, children, and the marriage. While not everyone who desires this kind of arrangement can negotiate it, it is worth at least a try. Persons all along the spectrum of skills and professions have discovered ways to work out a part-time employment pattern.

Another way is for each partner to commit something less than full time to career. Then each can use the balance of time for marital, child-rearing, and home-care interests (Stuart and Jacobson, 1985, p. 149). There are a few employment agencies attempting to place persons on twenty-five-hour work weeks. So far they have been more successful in placing women than men. But some men have discovered ways to make this work. For his book *Who Will Raise the Children?* James Levine located stories of some who were able to achieve this (1976, pp. 71–83).

Eric Barrett, an executive for the educational division of a large national corporation, requested a three-day work week. He wanted to have more time with his son. He also wanted his wife to have the opportunity to pursue a part-time career as a commercial artist. Eric's boss agreed to it, apparently because he was so valuable an employee.

Steve and Debbie Hoffman were co-owners and operators of a Manhattan printing business. The Hoffmans shared their work and the care of their two-year-old son, Michael. They achieved this by having one person at the office all the time. They made a special attempt to keep each other fully informed about all aspects of the work so that either or both could be responsible.

Hampshire College offered the opportunity to several faculty couples for each person to have a half-time appointment. This freed the couples to share child care and home life and to pursue yet other interests.

With the new information revolution, perhaps other options can be realized. Many a person could do the work required on a computer at home at a schedule of one's own convenience. This work could be transferred to a central office. This could make it possible for persons to be present and available to children when needed. The possibilities may be endless if a couple can become free inside to listen to their own needs. They may want to ask, "What style of working might make the most fulfilling life for us as individuals and as a family? What steps can we take to make our combined employment fit that dream?"

Unemployment

Up to this point we have described circumstances in which the couple had the free choice of whether or not to be employed. There are others who find themselves in a changing employment situation that is not of their choosing. They are involuntarily unemployed. Some of these persons are disabled, and thus face the possibility of permanent unemployment or great obstacles in gaining employment. Some have been fired or laid off and will be out of work until they find another job.

Dale was one of the latter. He recalls:

I had been in middle management of an aggressive, rapidly growing firm. At times I felt that we were too ruthless in our dealings with our employees when they were no longer useful to us. I was able to push through a few moderating changes, but for the most part my suggestions fell on deaf ears.

Little did I know that I was soon to become the victim of those very policies. Rather quickly our company went sour. Rumors of bankruptcy were flying around. Those at the top determined to cut our size very quickly, at every level. Unexpectedly and suddenly I was out!

I received some modest severance benefits, so I had a little time to work out something new. However, my financial obligations were such that I knew I had to do something quick.

The first few days felt like vacation at home. It had been so tense around the office that it was almost a relief to know that I was out. That quickly changed. It was followed by boredom and panic. Tension developed between my wife and me. We just didn't know what to say to each other. We both knew that the other was worried and upset. It was so hard to reach out to each other.

I dreaded meeting people at church or other gatherings. They'd ask if I'd found anything yet. For a while I wasn't even looking. And even when I was, it took time, lots of time. I resented being asked, and I resented having nothing to answer.

I felt paralyzed. It had been so long since I had looked for a job. Often firms had come to me! And now, here I was out job-begging. I didn't feel comfortable doing it, and I did it rather badly.

I guess I felt a certain shame. In my head, I knew that my being fired was no reflection on me. Still, in my gut, I had doubts. It was so hard to get going! I would have good ideas about people to contact. Then I would think of a thousand reasons not to pick up the telephone. I could put these calls off for days.

Because there were thousands of us laid off at the same time, my community had responded. Several agencies and at least one church offered job-hunting clinics or life/career-planning programs. Somehow I found it easier to go to those than to write my letters and make my calls. The ideas along with the support and encouragement of the other people somehow got me going.

I began to recognize this firing as a good thing. I hadn't been content there, but it was just too good a job to quit. Now that era was over; what next? What would I really love to do with my life? What would more truly express me? Maybe I couldn't find the exact thing, but if I knew more about me, I could give it a try. That's what I set out to discover.

As it happened, it turned out rather well. In time I did find a job, with a smaller company, where I could create more and administer less. This job was close to my personal ideal. It was even near enough that I didn't have to uproot my family from our home.

I can still remember how strange, how lonely, how frightening that jobless time was. How grateful I am for the caring people I met at that time! We saw each other through days that could have been even more tragic than they were.

Many people find themselves involuntarily jobless. Many more are marginally employed, with income far below their need. All of them live with the issues Dale faced. Some will experience them more acutely, because they won't have the broad background of experience, education, and skill that he had. Fortunate are those persons who find meaningful support systems to help them as individuals and families through such searching times.

Retirement

Men entering retirement may choose to be househusbands, if their wives are still employed. Or they may feel as if they are unemployed, but with this difference—there is a vagueness about the "employment" they should be seeking. Is it a hobby, volunteerism, or remunerative employment?

Both men and women find in retirement they must redefine themselves apart from their workplace and task. This may be a particularly acute issue if a person elects or is forced to take early retirement. What does one do with health, vigor, and skills when one has been released from the workplace?

Biblical Affirmations for Families with Employment Issues

With regard to the families we have described, we believe that biblical theology affirms the following:

Male and female are created in God's image, and part of that image is God's gift of creativity.

There is neither Jew nor Greek, male nor female, in God's loving family, and there are no set roles for male or female in a marriage. Roles can be freely chosen to provide the most creative environment possible for personal and community fulfillment.

God's call is to be, to relate, and to do. People have worth and dignity at all times, including those times when unemployment, frailty, or retirement may limit one's opportunity to do.

We Christians are citizens of two kingdoms, or cultures—an earthly one and a heavenly one that transcends culture's usual ways of doing things. Therefore the church is free to affirm the person who seeks a nontraditional role such as househusbanding.

How Some Churches Have Responded

As persons seek renegotiating of roles and tasks within marriage, at the very least the church should not be a barrier. The church should, rather, be a contributor to family strength, ready to offer whatever encouragement it can.

First Baptist Church of Boulder, Colorado, discovered two ways to respond to persons in these circumstances.

First, as part of their summer retreat program, they offered a weekend on "The Two-Career Couple." The group met from a Friday evening through Sunday noon under the leadership of a skilled retreat leader. She brought to the retreat a rich background. This included marriage enrichment experiences, familiarity with the Hall and Rowatt books mentioned earlier, and her own firsthand experience in a two-career marriage. Five couples participated.

When those who took part evaluated the weekend at its conclusion, they realized that it had been a difficult retreat to lead as well as to experience. The benefits varied from couple to couple. Future planners of retreats on this topic would be wise to explore not only common themes but ways in which each two-career couple is unique. Because of time pressures and the fatigue frequent with such couples, a leisurely pace with time for adequate rest and play should be provided. All agreed it was a vital topic that was worthy of discussion.

The second contribution by the Boulder Church came in response to an employment crisis in the community. For some years, the pastor had offered a life/career planning course of several sessions once or twice a year. He had been trained by Richard Bolles, author of *What Color Is Your Parachute?* and he conducted this course according to the model described in that book. A number of persons from the church and community and parents of children from the church preschool had participated in this course.

Then many employers, including the largest employer in the county, made major cutbacks. The pastor urged the church to respond by offering life/career planning groups free of charge to any who were out of work. A number of people offered help of various kinds. Some persons who had taken the course agreed to serve as registrars, hostesses, and small-group leaders. Others agreed to spread word of the groups among churches, agencies, newspapers, and employers who were dismissing workers. Still others created a hospitable atmosphere by providing coffee and home-baked treats. A businessman provided funds for all the materials.

Over the next several months, four groups were held, each meeting weekly over a six- or seven-week period. The participants learned how to plan and investigate both their own gifts and the potential job market by Bolles's methods. They also lent much encouragement, support, and information to one another. When the need decreased, more than a hundred persons had participated in this program. That was a small part of the thousands who were out of work. Yet the individual discoveries that resulted and the community awareness that a church responded to this need were rich gains.

In another part of the country, a pastor and church found a way to deal with another work-related issue as they lent aid to a couple undergoing stress because of employment problems.

When her husband was temporarily out of work, Ann (not her real name) was delighted to gain employment on the custodial staff of a local educational institution. She was pleased to find a job with an adequate pay scale and a benefit plan that included medical and hospitalization insurance for her family.

Rather soon after she began work, however, she faced difficulties. She didn't agree with what she saw as rather low standards of performance. Moreover, she was uncomfortable with the sexual innuendos and flirtation imposed on her and other female employees. She was unwilling to go along with disappearing to an unseen place to play cards for an hour or two on employer time. Since she refused to participate in such practices, she was harassed even more. At times she found a room she had cleaned had been messed up to make her appear incompetent.

The tension heightened when her supervisor gave her an unsatisfactory report in one of her early job evaluations. If unchallenged and allowed to stand, that could have led to her dismissal.

In distress she came to her pastor and told him of her work troubles. He listened with care and then rallied support. Among those he contacted were representatives of the women's resource center in the community and the women's committee at the institution. (The church had members who were on both of these women's support groups.) With the help and advice gained from these sources, they devised a strategy.

They chose to attempt to work with the institution itself. Ann was advised to keep careful records of work and incidents. She appealed the unsatisfactory job report and asked for particulars. The process was slow and laborious. There were many communications, hearings, committee meetings. Eventually, her record was cleared. She was recognized as a valuable employee. Her employment was not destroyed by an "old boy" system.

That would be reason enough to celebrate, but there was even more. Sensitized by what she had experienced, Ann agreed to serve on the women's concern committee of that institution. As a result, she willingly took training courses and seminars that were offered on work management or sexual harassment issues. She has made it easier for others who come into the same work force and has contributed to an improved employment environment.

Appropriate Care

Here are some ways that churches can respond to those couples and families whose lives are impacted by changing employment patterns:

• Offer life/career planning groups to help couples develop a mutual career strategy or help out-of-work persons focus on job targets.

• Create job-hunting support groups to help jobless people continue in the lonely, discouraging task of job-hunting. Some churches have found ways to mobilize church resources for job hunters. Informal mention of job needs in newsletters or at church groups has led to job leads. One church maintains a "job bank"—a listing of known opportunities. Networks of persons who have access to their employers' needs have been helpful.

• Provide sensitive support to those anticipating retirement and in the early stages of retirement. Sympathetic, encouraging listening is a starting place. Other opportunities to be supportive might grow out of such openness.

• Offer a couples group that explores changing roles in marriage and develops skills to renegotiate appropriate roles in marriage.

• Take a "church vacation" together as a group of couples/families with similar interests. Busy people might appreciate opportunities to think through priorities, develop time-management skills, and learn how to relax and play. Retreats might combine much-needed rest with consideration of timely topics. One such topic might be how to find spiritual replenishment amid the pressures of work and family living.

• Explore the issue of competent, compassionate care for children. Perhaps a total day-care program or an after-school program may be needed. Possibly a referral system of child care facilities might suffice.

• Initiate discussion groups that directly address such themes as two-career couples, househusbanding, or employment issues.

• Facilitate informal linkages between couples living with similar problems. Even an acquaintance with one other couple going through the same things might be a very special gift.

• Face, discuss, and plan strategies to deal with the changed situation in volunteerism. On the one hand, the increased employment of women means that they have less time to give. On the other hand, many women are developing leadership and executive skills. Such skills could be more creatively used by some churches. Are all offices, boards, tasks of your church open to persons of both sexes?

• Reexamine the church's own employment policies—including those of agencies and institutions created by the church. Does the church show sensitivity and flexibility so that two-career couples can flourish? In particular, is it showing sensitivity to the small but growing number of clergy couples? Are they being given opportunities to serve together or in proximity to each other?

Resources and References

Beer, William R. 1983. *Househusbands: Men and Housework in American Families*. South Hadley, Mass.: Bergin and Garvey Publishers.

Bird, Caroline. 1979. *The Two-Paycheck Marriage*. New York: Pocket Books.

Bolles, Richard N. *The Three Boxes of Life and How to Get Out of Them*, *The Quick Job Hunting Map*, and *What Color Is Your Parachute?* All are published in constantly updated editions by Ten Speed Press, Berkeley, Calif. Bolles's organization, the National Career Development Project (Box 379, Walnut Creek, CA 94956), offers regional training experiences to those who wish to offer life/career planning groups.

Brin, Douglas. 1984. "Confessions of a Househusband." *Parents*, March, pp. 78–80.

Carro, Geraldine. 1983. "Stay-Home Fathers' Superkids." *Psychology Today*, January, p. 71.

Cohen, Richard. 1984. "Men Sharing." *Ms*, August, pp. 74–75.

Curtis, Jean. 1976. *Working Mothers*. Garden City, N.Y.: Doubleday & Co.

Hall, Francine, and Douglas T. Hall. 1979. *The Two-Career Couple*. Reading, Mass.: Addison-Wesley Publishing Co.

Halloran, Daniel F. 1985. "Where the Buck Stops." *America*, Dec. 28, pp. 461–464.

Holmstrom, Lynda Lytle. 1972. *The Two-Career Family*. Cambridge, Mass.: Schenkman Publishing Co.

Lamb, Michael E., and Abraham Sagi, eds. 1983. *Fatherhood and Family Policy*. Hillsdale, N.J.: Lawrence Erlbaum Associates.

Levine, James A. 1979. *Who Will Raise the Children?* Philadelphia: J. B. Lippincott Co.

McGrady, Mike. 1975. *The Kitchen Sink Papers: My Life as a House-husband.* Garden City, N.Y.: Doubleday & Co.

Mollenkott, Virginia Ramey. 1977. *Women, Men, and the Bible.* Nashville: Abingdon Press.

Olson, Richard P. 1984. *Changing Male Roles in Today's World.* Valley Forge, Pa.: Judson Press.

Pogrebin, Letty Cottin. 1980. *Growing Up Free: Raising Your Children in the 80's.* New York: McGraw-Hill Book Co.

Rowatt, G. Wade, Jr., and Mary Jo Rowatt. 1980. *The Two-Career Marriage.* Philadelphia: Westminster Press.

Scanzoni, Letha, and Nancy Hardesty. 1974. *All We're Meant to Be.* Waco, Tex.: Word Books.

Stuart, Richard B., and Barbara Jacobson. 1985. *Second Marriage: Make It Happy! Make It Last!* New York: W. W. Norton & Co.

U.S. Bureau of the Census. 1986. *Women in the American Economy.* Current Population Reports, Series P-23, no. 146. Washington, D.C.: U.S. Government Printing Office.

_____. 1987. *Statistical Abstract of the United States: 1988* (108th ed.). Washington, D.C.: U.S. Government Printing Office.

3

The Single-Parent Family

Let's begin with the story of a woman named Susan.

I am a woman in my early thirties, a single parent, divorced. This is a place that I never expected to be in my life. It has been three years since my separation and one year since my divorce and the custody hearing for our daughter.

I was raised in a small town in a middle-class family, where the norm was to marry early and have children. It was expected that one would stay married and be happy and content—an uncomplicated life. What happened is very difficult to explain in a few short paragraphs.

I always did what I thought was right—what would make every-body happy. In the process of doing that, I began to lose myself. My emotions began to fade, along with my sense of self. I knew that there had to be change. I prayed a lot then, and cried a lot too.

After a lot of changes, a lot of decisions, the consequences for me were difficult. My husband and I separated. I moved back to my home state to finish college. My husband filed for divorce and wanted custody of our daughter. The custody battle lasted for one year. This was a very painful time—a time when I couldn't even go to God. From the day that my daughter was born, I had thanked God in every prayer for giving me this child to care for, to guide through life. That this purpose in my life was being threatened was unbelievable. Yet it was happening.

I had very few resources and very few emotional supports. I did have a very caring sister and an attorney whom I could put my trust in, who later became a friend. And I had myself.

Looking back now, I can easily see that in having myself, I had God. I was so blind to that then. My prayers seemed so hollow that I ended them. My sense of being was so threatened that I had thoughts of ending that. Through that time, nothing was constant.

But God was with me and gave the beginnings of strength. I was in so much pain—but feeling emotion again! I began to pray again, and my prayers slowly became filled.

I was granted full custody. My daughter flies to Florida frequently to visit her father and is with him for the summer. I miss her so much then. There are still a lot of painful times.

Susan's experience introduces us to another family group, the single-parent family. This is an important and rapidly growing part of the American family scene. According to a U.S. Census Bureau study of marital status and living arrangements released in March 1988, single-parent families composed 24.3% of all family groups, compared to 19.7% in 1980 and 11.9% in 1970. Or to express this increase in another manner, while in 1970 roughly 1 in 8 families with children under 18 present was a single-parent family, in 1988 the ratio was 1 in 4. Throughout this period, mothers headed 90% of these families and fathers approximately 10%.

According to the March 1988 report of the Census Bureau, 33% of single-parent families are headed by a divorced mother, 28% by a never-married mother, 22% by a separated mother, and 6% by a widow. Divorced fathers head 6% of single-parent homes, separated fathers 3%, never-married fathers 2%, and widowers 1%.

There are three ways one becomes a single parent: through death; through divorce; and through unwed parenthood. We shall look at each of these in turn. And then we shall explore some of the basic issues common to most single-parent families.

Single Parenthood Through Divorce

What is the process by which a divorce occurs? Constance Ahrons has noted five transitions.

First, there occurs "individual cognition." One partner senses that something is acutely wrong. This may be mostly on a feeling level or it may be on a level of conscious thought. Perhaps this partner is depressed, or possibly the conflict level has risen a great deal.

The second transition is "family metacognition." The family members begin to realize that the marriage is disintegrating. The couple may talk seriously about separating and perhaps discuss this possibility with the children.

The third transition is "separation." At this point one partner moves out of the household. This may be a long transitional period. Sometimes the partners reconcile and reunite briefly because of feelings of ambivalence or possibly guilt over their children's distress. The family is in a state of flux: What is the status of this family and who are the members? Such questions seem to be quite unresolved.

Transition four is "family reorganization." A difficult issue at this point is redefining the coparenting relationship. The couple have the stressful task of trying to learn to separate spouse roles from parental roles. They terminate the spouse roles but continue the parental roles. At the same time they need to negotiate a redefinition of these parental roles. Often there is still so much residual anger and hurt that this seems a nearly impossible task. Yet it is one that must be done if they are to function effectively in the future.

Part of this reorganization involves decisions about custody. Will there be joint custody? (In many states, joint custody is presumed unless reasons to the contrary can be presented to the court.) Does joint custody mean that the children spend equal time in each household? If so, what will be the division of time and how will it be arranged? When the children are with one parent, what decisions reside with that parent and what decisions should be shared?

The fifth transition is "family redefinition." If one parent is leaving and not entering into any continuing relationship with the children, the family closes ranks without that parent. The term "single-parent family" in descriptions of divorced families contains the assumption that divorce results in one parent leaving the family system (Ahrons 1983, pp. 107–111).

Ahrons notes that this style of coping with family reorganization may produce much individual stress and family dysfunction. "Noncustodial fathers with infrequent post divorce contact with their children were reported to be more depressed . . . more dissatisfied with their relationship with their children, and more stressed regarding role loss. Sole custody mothers were more depressed and over burdened by the responsibilities resulting from the role overload. Children with very limited or no father contact suffered the most severe developmental and emotional distress" (Ahrons 1983, pp. 111–112).

And so, given that a divorce has taken place, Ahrons argues for the creation of interrelated maternal and paternal households, if possible. This requires a new term, a "binuclear family system," a family system with two nuclei (p. 112). Sometimes families find this arrangement impossible. There may be too much anger. Still, if possible, this pattern seems best. Though the research on this topic has been limited to small samples, it indicates that the child's sense of loss is less if contact can be maintained with both parents.

So far we have explored the stressful transitions facing the family going through divorce. What about the individuals involved? Bruce Fisher was divorced and then carefully studied the inner experience of recovery. He suggests there are fifteen issues to be faced within oneself in recovering from the trauma of a divorce (1981, pp. 8–19):

1. Denial. No one expects to be divorced, so it is difficult to admit to self and to others.

2. Loneliness. Some say this is the greatest loneliness one may ever expect to experience.

3. Rejection or guilt. One may have been the "dumper" (the one who elected to leave) and experience guilt. Or one may have been the "dumpee" (the one left) and experience rejection.

4. Grief. One mourns the death of a relationship, a lifestyle, an ideal, a dream, a companionship.

5. Anger. There will likely occur a rage, the intensity of which may shock the person who experiences it. But it helps lead to the next step.

6. Letting go. There is the task of freeing oneself from the "emotional corpse" (that is, the dead relationship as far as its being a marital partnership). One discovers the unfruitfulness of trying to maintain a relationship that holds no promise and chooses to put one's energy elsewhere.

7. Self-esteem. A divorce is a blow to one's self-esteem. One may feel unworthy of friendship, of love, even of jobs for which one applies. Attention and effort may need to be directed at rebuilding one's self-esteem.

8. Friendships. Many divorced persons discover some old friendships can no longer be maintained. New friendships have to be formed.

9. Leftovers. One discovers those hangups, difficulties, neuroses that one has "left over" from childhood, youth, and perhaps the former love relationship.

10. Love. One usually leaves a marriage feeling unloved and unlovable, and shouting "never again." One aspect of healing is the recovery of healthy self-love and confidence that one can love others as well.

11. Trust. When a marriage relationship ends, a person often has a "love wound." This is a hurt so great that trusting anyone is difficult. When healing starts, one takes small steps toward risking emotional closeness again.

12. Sexuality. Sexual needs go on. For a time a divorced person may experience a total lack of interest in sex. Then possibly one may experience obsession with sex. Then perhaps there is a time of more balanced awareness of one's sexual needs.

13. Responsibility. One may have been overdependent or underdependent in the previous relationship. The person needs to achieve self-independence. Then one can explore possible relationships in which two healthily independent persons are also willing to give and receive care from each other.

14. Singleness. Many persons have never experienced singleness. They went from family of origin to marriage. Discovering that one can survive as a single, even be happy, is an important step. Future decisions can be made from strength.

15. Freedom. One becomes free to choose singleness or a new relationship. A person also finds the freedom to be himself or herself, not shackled by unrecognized needs or by compulsions to please others.

These issues do not arise neatly in sequence. Some have more importance for some persons than for others. Certain people never face them all. A new crisis (such as a court hearing, a fight, the awareness that one's former mate is dating or has married) can throw one back into issues thought resolved. But these are inner problems that every divorcing person has to face. The process takes time. Many estimate that from six months to three years will pass before, as one person put it, "You lift up, kind of."

The experience of divorce is also a profound spiritual struggle. For some, the struggle is almost entirely negative. It may be a sense of abandonment and of feeling judged and rejected by church friends. This may confirm guilt and fear that one has been abandoned by God as well. For others there is a positive element of spiritual growth as one is thrust into an insecure void. Some persons then reach out. One woman recalled, "My divorce was a religious experience." She claimed the promises of God to help, sustain, comfort, and forgive. And though she had to leave one church and find another, she found those promises to be fulfilled for her.

And what is the children's experience? Undoubtedly, they face many of the same issues as their parents. Their questions must include these: (1) Am I going to be deprived of one of my parents, or can I have some relationship with both (and do I want it with the one who left)? (2) If Mom and Dad still have contact with each other at all, are they going to stop fighting? (3) Is my life going to be disrupted in yet other ways—moving away from neighborhood, friends, school, and church, or being separated from brothers or sisters?

Single Parenthood Through Death

Some persons become part of single-parent families because of death. According to psychologists who have carefully observed this process, there are three phases of early widowhood: impact, recoil, and recovery.

The first stage, *impact*, is that period of catastrophe when the blow of death is first absorbed. It can last from the moment of death to as long as six months later. Persons may remember this as a time of numbness. Many widows/widowers stay in character during this period. They may be gracious, poised, and efficient through the early days of mourning, including the funeral. Widowed persons may have to make many decisions and adjustments well before they are in a position to do so wisely. The second stage, *recoil*, is when shock is replaced by the stark knowledge that the death is real. The loss is permanent. Charlotte, a widow of six years, describes it this way. "It's difficult to describe, but after a couple of months of limbo in which getting through each day is a miracle, you know, really and awfully, that your husband is dead. When I finally stopped listening for his steps on the stairs, then it all became real to me" (Lindsay 1981, p. 4).

Loewinsohn points out that there are three emotions that can cause great anguish during recoil: guilt ("If only I had . . . "); denial of reality (choosing to live in the past rather than in the painful present); and anger (at life, God, the deceased, others around one, or at self). She points out that these emotions are interrelated. "If you can get in touch with the anger that may rest beneath your feelings of guilt and your denial of reality, if you can give yourself permission to feel the anger and work through it, you may find it possible to begin to say good-bye" (Loewinsohn 1979, pp. 69–77).

In time, there comes a third stage of grieving—*recovery*. This comes when one can accept the death, grant the dead spouse a place in history. One can then say good-bye to the dead person and get on with the business of living. It comes when one has discovered how to live on one's own. The bereaved has learned how to fill the painful gaps left by the deceased and how to find joys and pleasures in living. There may be occasional returns to lonely, tear-filled times, but these will be less frequent. More days will have life and joy in them.

As regards this grieving process, many persons testify that churches have well-established means of being helpful during *impact*—responding with visits, food, flowers, cards, attendance at the funeral. These persons felt little support, however, during recoil. This stage may take months or years. One perceptive widow recalled, "When my husband first died, I was absolutely surrounded by love and compassion. Maybe it was too much. For a time I was so pampered, I wasn't even dealing with my grief. Then suddenly it was gone. And there was nobody who even wanted to listen when I felt the need to keep talking about him." And a distressed widower told me, "I'm not through talking about her, but it seems that everyone else is."

Children in the family have the additional fear of losing the other parent. They may make demands of presence and attention at a time when that bereaved parent is most vulnerable.

Single Parenthood Through Unwed Parenting

In spite of the difficulties, some unmarried individuals succeed in adopting children. They may be granted custody of hard-to-place children who are older or have mental or physical disabilities. Such adults may find the transition from childlessness to the responsibility for time, care, finances, and parenting skills coming upon them rather abruptly.

Many more unmarried people become parents through pregnancy and childbirth. The U.S. Census Bureau noted 709,000 births to unmarried women in the United States in the year that ended in June 1987. This included 583,000 to never-married mothers and 126,000 born to widows or divorcées. It further noted that out-of-wedlock births to mothers eighteen to twenty-four account for one of every five white babies and almost three out of four births to black women (U.S. Bureau of the Census 1988).

Margaret C. Simms, an Urban Institute researcher, commented that young women nowadays are giving serious thought to whether they want to marry after becoming pregnant. They may see the father as a bad marriage risk. They may also know how unstable have been the marriages of others who married because of pregnancy.

Martha Burt, another Urban Institute researcher, added, "For teens, it is actually detrimental in the long run to get married. Married teens are more likely to drop out of school and it decreases the ability of both boys and girls to support themselves. Also, they are likely to have more children more quickly. The upshot is that marriage is not the solution, given the other problems of poverty and low skills" (Reported in *Kansas City Star*, June 26, 1986).

Given the more readily available birth control methods, it is not clear why the rate of births to unmarried women is so high. Various factors can be noted. One is that there seems to be less public disapproval over unmarried children having babies. Others note that some persons conceive and raise a child to gain some sense of legitimacy not otherwise felt (Bustanoby 1985, p. 98). There also seems to be much ignorance, carelessness, and lack of knowledge of, or lack of access to adequate birth control methods. One study reveals that among the unmarried 15- to 19-year-olds, 90 percent of all the pregnancies were unintended (Alan Guttmacher Institute 1976, pp. 16–17). All observers agree that the situation of those "who became parents before they became adults" (ibid., p. 5) has many tragic overtones. Arthur A. Campbell once wrote:

> The timing of the first birth is of crucial strategic importance in the lives of young women, because the need to take care of a baby limits severely their ability to take advantage of opportunities that might have changed their lives for the better. In this regard, the problems posed by births to unmarried women are especially serious. The girl who has an illegitimate child at the age of 16 suddenly has 90 percent of her life's script written for her. She will probably drop out of school; even if someone else in her family helps to take care of the baby, she will probably not be able to find a steady job that pays enough to provide for herself and her child; she may feel impelled to marry someone she might not otherwise have chosen. Her life choices are few, and most of them are bad. Had she been able to delay the first child, her prospects might have been quite different, assuming that she would have had opportunities to continue her education, improve her vocational skills, find a job, marry someone she wanted to marry, and have a child when she and her husband were ready for it. Also, the child would have been born under quite different circumstances and might have grown up in a stable family environment" (Campbell 1968, quoted in Guttmacher Institute 1976, p. 18).

In addition, mothers in their early teens have a greater risk of maternal death, toxemia, hemorrhage, spontaneous abortion, low birth weight, and infant death than do mothers 20 to 24 years of age. The young mothers are apt not to graduate from high school or have work experience before the birth of their first child. Teen mothers face greater risk of unemployment and welfare dependency. And if they seek to contract a marriage with the father of their child, they live with the harsh reality that three in five pregnant teen brides are divorced within six years (ibid., pp. 21–28).

What are the unique stress experiences for never-married persons entering parenthood, either through adoption or birthing? Their stress comes from a different point than their divorced or widowed single-parent counterparts. In the case of the latter, the experience was the subtraction of a family member who potentially could share the care-giving tasks. For the never-married parent, the experience is the addition of a person needing care. When some never-married adoptive single parents were asked about their adjustments to their new role they spoke of lack of time, physical exhaustion, the "twenty-four-hour-a-dayness" of the job. In addition they mentioned the financial adjustments and learning to converse with someone else at mealtimes. And, even more, they spoke of the need to discover patience and skill in dealing with one's temper (Bustanoby 1985, pp. 111–112). Quite likely birthing unmarried single parents would have a similar list.

The Common Ongoing Tasks of the Single Parent

Hanson and Sporakowski, family life authorities, regret that in the past most studies of the single family were built on a "deficit model." Such studies attempted to "prove" that single-parent families were unhealthy situations in which to live and grow. These authors are heartened to see a more positive approach. "Family social scientists are starting to isolate the many factors that place these [single-parent] families at risk and are beginning to suggest the ways that society can assist them" (1986, p. 7). They suggest, then, that single-parent families can be healthy. Nevertheless, at many points they are "at risk." What are the tasks of the single parent, and what are the points at which she or he is at risk?

Role Flexibility

The single parent needs to develop a flexibility of roles. For the male, this may mean developing many domestic and child care skills in order to provide all that his child needs. Said one father, "I wasn't a full parent, [in] that I was only around in minor ways when it came to all the duties of taking care of them—arranging for doctors, dentists and baby sitters, [and] decisions if they needed new shoes" (Hogan et al. 1983, p. 121). For the female, the role change may be an evaluation of her wage-earning capacity. She may need to make decisions and take steps to improve that earning capacity. Adults must attempt to spread themselves thinner, take on new roles, learn new skills to provide what their children need.

Child Custody

Both custodial and noncustodial single parents need to come to grips with the meaning of that aspect of their respective roles.

In a study of single fathers, it was noted that fathers arrived at custody of their children in one of three ways: (1) as conciliatory negotiators—those who gained custody of their children as a result of amicable discussions and joint decisions; (2) as hostile seekers—those who fought for custody of their children, often to punish ex-wives for some disapproved activity; and (3) as passive acceptors who had been deserted by their wives (Risman 1986, p. 97). The means by which one arrives at custody of children will influence one's attitude and satisfaction in that role. Likewise, persons might arrive at noncustody in the same manner, by negotiating, conflicting, or abandoning. The means by which one came to that place will influence one's attitude and performance as a noncustodial parent.

Time Management

The single parent attempts the complex time-management plan needed to accomplish the parenting responsibilities. Robert Weiss notes that in every household there are three "task packages": (1) income production, (2) home maintenance, and (3) child care, both instrumental and affectional. When a couple are married, they somehow divide these three task packages. For the single parent, all three packages fall on her or him (Weiss 1979, pp. 47–48). Single parents will face this virtually impossible time crunch in any of a number of ways (or combination of ways):

• By ignoring and simplifying many household tasks ("What's ironing?")

• By eliminating or reducing activities, groups, and associations that had once been personally satisfying (including, perhaps, church activities)

• By recruiting family members to take part in the family work

• By facing irrational self-expectations and deciding what is central and most important (Murdock 1980, pp. 31–36).

Yet another part of time management is negotiating the conflict between family needs and personal needs. One needs privacy, space, time, social life (possibly including dating life), and activities that contribute to one's spiritual renewal. As one parent asked, "How do I avoid the extremes of living solely for my children and winding up resenting them, or living for myself and treating my kids like abandoned children? How do I find balance in my life?"

Economic Issues

In addition, the single parent needs to deal with economic stressors and with equally difficult financial management issues. Hogan et al. (1983, pp. 123–127) note that three related economic changes are common to the single-parent family.

1. Income usually decreases with the loss of an adult wage earner. And since the custodial wage earner is frequently the female (who, sadly, is likely to be the lesser earner), the loss of income may be severe. In the case of divorce, material goods may be divided. All this leads to downward economic status for the family.

2. The sources of family income may change. Perhaps some of the family income will come from some form of government subsidy (Aid to Dependent Children, or welfare, or food stamps, or lunch program, for example). Perhaps some of the income will be child-support payments from the noncustodial parent. Both of these sources of income may be problematical to the family at times. The government sub-

sidies are subject to bureaucratic procedures, delays, changes, and regulations.

Child-support payments can be both rather small and irregular. In 1978, child support was awarded to only 59 percent of the divorced women with dependent children. Of those who were awarded payments by the courts, only about one half received full payments. A fourth received partial payments, and another fourth received no payments at all.

3. The family may temporarily or permanently have to change its living standard. They may have to move into low-income housing or a grandparent's household.

The single parent needs to develop complex financial management skills. The questions must be posed both for oneself and for one's family: What are the necessities? What are "luxuries" that we can do without? Which do we treasure and enjoy so much that we will spend some of our scarce money resources for them?

The single parent also needs to learn how to be a resource broker. One will have to discover what services are available for single parents in the community. Is there child care for working parents? opportunity for education and other job training or improvement? flexible-time employment? counseling and/or remedial help for children or a parent? Are there financial-aid resources that can help stretch the family's too-thin budget? If so, where are these services? How does one apply, qualify, and obtain such aid?

A single parent will therefore need to learn how to deal with bureaucracies—governmental, private agency, educational, and church. And one will need to develop skills in application writing, patience, persistence, negotiation, time investment, and flexibility that are needed in dealing with such bureaucracies.

Parenting Style

Then, too, persons will need to evolve an appropriate parent-child relationship, including parental leadership and discipline. Persons who have been both married and single parents have reflected that they evolved a different parent-child relationship in the single-parent family. They note there is often less "generational distance," less parental authority, and more family democracy. Many single parents invite their children into partnership in doing the family work, in sharing the responsibilities, in earning and spending the money, and hence in family decision-making.

Sometimes there is a near role-reversal. For example, the parent may be very tired or feel discouraged or frightened about the family's circumstances. The children may behave almost as parent to the parent for a time, offering consolation, support, and care. Other parents sense that they have become more of a peer to their children, a sort of big sister or brother. Many point out that children learn new responsibilities (such as caring for siblings) and new skills (possibly cooking, homemaking, yard work) and become more independent and self-reliant as a result.

When this mutual interdependency works, families experience a real sense of loyalty and teamwork. When it does not, and there is resulting bickering, disobedience, delinquency, and fighting, the single parent carries an extra-heavy load.

Single parents have a distinct and important issue to face in all of this. What is the appropriate parental distance, leadership, discipline, and self-care? In what way can we build family life so we achieve our family responsibilities and individual growth and development?

In Summary, the Challenge

We have been attempting to describe entry into the single-parent family status and some of the issues these families face. Perhaps an obstetrics nurse, married and the mother of two preschool children, summarized it best. Said she: "My husband is a great help with our children. And we have a good support group. There are fine church programs for us, relatives who offer us emotional support, and a good day-care center that we can afford with our combined incomes. And yet there are times when raising these children takes everything we've both got. So when I go to work and see these single parents giving birth and intending to raise the child by themselves, I want to say, 'You're out of your mind!'"

Out of their minds or not, millions enter single parenthood. Some do it willingly, and some have it thrust upon them. Quite likely there will be help needed. Sometimes the needs will be greater and more desperate than at other times. But the welfare of individuals, families, and our nation is at stake. Who will respond to help these families be strong and competent?

A Theological Response

In an article exploring the various informal support systems available for single parents, Nancy Wells Gladow and Margaret P. Ray make the following observation: "Very little is known about churches as a source of social support for single parents. The only recent research available on single parents and religious institutions showed few single parents utilizing this potential source of support. One might expect that since churches would be somewhat unaccepting of either divorce or pregnancy outside of marriage, they would do little to provide meaningful support for single parents. Whether the church is an important source of social support for low income single parents today is unknown" (Gladow and Ray 1986, pp. 114–115).

They perceive that the church's moral judgments on divorce and nonmarital pregnancy would inhibit the church's compassion for single parents. Many single-parent families think so too, and consequently do not look to the church for personal support.

The elements of a theology big enough to propel church people into helping single parents in their important tasks of child-rearing are close at hand in the Bible.

For example, "Religion that is pure and undefiled before God . . . is this: to visit orphans and widows in their affliction" (James 1:27). Would it be too farfetched to suspect that not only widows but all attempting to rear children without a spouse's partnership might be included in this verse?

The Bible continues to speak of widows and calls for compassionate support to widowed families. These families were protected with special legislation and were seen as persons for whom God cared especially. The early New Testament church had programs to provide care for widows. In fact, it appears that they offered so much care that they overextended themselves and had to limit their support only to those that met the test of "real" widows (see 1 Tim. 5:3–16). "Widows" may have been an office with particular responsibilities in the early church. Thus the care-giving was mutual.

The prophet, the psalmist, and Jesus all spoke of God's special concern for the poor. (And single-parent families are an important segment of the poor of our nation. Half of all single-parent families live below the poverty level.)

Still other objects of God's compassion and of Jesus' particular attention and tenderness are children. "It is not the will of my Father . . . that one of these little ones should perish."

With uncanny awareness that no family (one-parent or two-parent) is really sufficient in itself for its complicated tasks, the New Testament writers frequently refer to the church as family. It is to be a community where family love, nurture, strength, support, and sharing take place among its members.

It appears that for part of his life Jesus lived in a single-parent family! Joseph is never present again after the Temple encounter, when Jesus was twelve, while Mary continued as an important influence on his life. Followers of Jesus, realizing this, may be led to compassion for the struggles she must have had and to celebration of the gift of family support she gave to our Lord.

The Bible offers a mandate to be advocate for those who have less than their share of power and more than their share of needs. The single-parent family is often among those.

Appropriate Care

A church that has decided to be involved can offer much support from the resources it already has at hand. Gladow and Ray have suggested (1986, p. 114) that social support has three components: (1) emotional support that lets persons understand that they are cared for and appreciated; (2) esteem support, helping persons know they are valued and valuable; and (3) network support, providing a group of people with mutual care for one another, providing information and other aid for solving problems. They suggest further that this type of support may be experienced in three ways: (1) formal—from professional helping relationships, such as counselors and agency workers; (2) structured informal—the by-product of involvement in such structured group activities as PTA, churches, lodges, unions, and clubs; and (3) informal social support from relationships with kin, neighbors, friends, and so on.

The church could be involved in offering support on all levels and in each of the ways mentioned. Some of the support a church might offer could include:

• Personal counsel and growth groups for persons experiencing divorce

• Counsel and groups for persons who have lost a spouse or parent to death

• Parenting skills groups

• Single-parent groups

We interviewed a number of single parents about what they would like from the church. Their answers fell mostly into the categories of the structured informal and informal support. Here are some of their comments:

> "I'd like a hug now and then. I'm not a leper, and I'm not after your husband [wife]."
> "Include single persons among whose whom you invite to a dinner party; include my family in family get-togethers."
> "Invite my family to share a holiday with you. Whether we can accept or not, the invitation feels wonderful!"
> "Develop a church skill bank, where persons could exchange skills we have for those we don't have but need, in order to function as a family. This would be useful for other than single-parent families."

"Give single parents assertiveness training, so they can communicate with
schools, agencies, and any other group to whom they need to present
their case."

"When children make gifts at church school, let the child make two if the
parents live apart."

"Parents who are not employed outside the home can offer to be contact
parents for emergencies involving children whose parents work. This
would be useful to all employed parents."

"Offers of child care are always appreciated. I may want to clean my house
or just be alone for a few hours."

"I enjoy potluck suppers for either single parents or all parents, where we
get to talk with one another and build up our network of acquaintances
and friends."

"Ask me for help in the church life once in a while. It probably needs to be a
short-term task, since my time is limited. But I like to give to persons
and organizations from whom I have received."

In addition, the church can be sensitive to the harsh economic
realities that many single-parent families face. This sensitivity may
express itself in a number of ways:

A church can examine its assumptions about how much money children
and youths can afford for church recreational outings.

A church can use its mutual-aid or discretionary fund to help single families
over difficult financial crises.

A church can be an advocate for services to single parents among private
and public agencies in the community.

A church leader can help single families be aware of benefits for which they
might qualify.

Thus the church can witness to a faithful, loving God who sustains
each of us, whatever our need, through our times of overwhelming
responsibilities, whatever those responsibilities may be.

And church leaders can communicate an understanding that the
single family can be a strong, stable family unit. Two-parent families
are not automatically effective, nor are single-parent families automatically ineffective. E. E. Lemasters, a professor of social work, has
written, "The one parent family has not proven to be psychologically
dysfunctional—its main problems are socioeconomic. Our society has
never properly organized for the one parent family" (Dalke 1977, p.
73). One single parent said, "I would love to be a part of a church that
said to me, 'I believe in you and your ability to function as a single
parent, and I will offer you help and support where you want it.' Don't
say to me, 'You poor thing, you deficit family!'"

Suzanne Stewart (1978, p. 53) commented that when asked, "If you
could give only one bit of advice to a parent rearing children alone,
what would it be?" she responded, "Without hesitation, I can answer,
'Become part of a church family. You'll need their support.'"

How Churches Have Responded

Here are two examples of how churches respond to single-parent families. The first is a rather small church. To discern its ministry, we pick up the story of Susan, who introduced us to this theme.

The time for adjustment came after the divorce. I was very vulnerable at this time. I wanted to fit in again and to have a sense of order back in my life. At the same time, I didn't want to be approached, pressured. My attorney had become my friend, so when he suggested his church, I trusted that it would be a safe place. Reluctantly, I went. I felt comfortable, welcomed, yet not pressured. . . .

The pastor made it clear to me that my daughter and I were welcome in church and at Sunday school. I felt that my ideas and thoughts were respected in Sunday school. We fit.

The first few Sundays that we went, as I sat with my arm around my daughter singing a hymn or listening to the choir, I found myself with tears in my eyes. The sense of order that this church had so easily put into my life overwhelmed me. It seemed as though everything else would fall into place. The simplicity of it all in such a complicated thing as life left me full of wonder and feeling connected again.

Susan's pastor saw this primarily as an act of lay ministry by Susan's attorney, who is also a deacon in the church. He offered care for her in her most pressing times of need. Then he invited her to his spiritual community. This relationship formed the bridge that made the life of the church available to her. The pastor offered her some spiritual counsel and support. For the most part, she set her own agenda and worked on the issues she selected. As she mentioned in describing her pilgrimage, these were issues of identity as a person, as a parent (and as a person who could lose custodial parenthood), and as a child of God. A low-pressure, accepting church community did the rest. The church and its ongoing Sunday school classes provided the support community that Susan wanted.

The other example comes from the Third Baptist Church of St. Louis, Missouri. Some years ago, when two divorced members of that church married each other, they made a decision. Don and Maggie Coplen had received much love and support in church-sponsored (mostly Roman Catholic) singles groups. They decided to give back some of that love by helping found a singles ministry in their church.

Their first effort was to offer a seminar lasting several weeks for persons who had recently become single. They recall that while this was not an unqualified success, they did learn some valuable lessons. For one thing, after once including both widowed and divorced persons in the same group, they now offer separate groups. Another issue was developing trust and comfort with the level of sharing that can happen in such groups. Some participants were uncomfortable about revealing their feelings with persons who might be their fellow church members for years to come. As the groups have grown, persons come from both inside and outside the church as the "grapevine" lets other interested people know of available, inexpensive, helpful groups. This broader mix provides a setting where deep sharing can occur.

The program has developed so that it offers four alternatives: (1) One continues to be the adjustment seminar for the newly singled—alternating between divorced and widowed persons. (2) A second is entitled "When Your Relationship Ends." This is a divorce and personal growth seminar based on the work of Bruce Fisher, who was mentioned earlier. They have adapted this program, however, to include their own spiritual convictions and to give participants opportunities for integrating their own spiritual insights. (3) The third is "The Fully Alive Experience: A Group Experience in Fully Human and Christian Living." This utilizes an audiotaped program and group-response material (Powell and Brady 1980). The Coplens have found it a good follow-up to the divorce seminar. It could also be a beneficial program for other segments of the church population. (4) A fourth option deals with "Building Healthy Healing Relationships." The leaders are currently putting together a program on singleness to precede this. The focus of the new program will be helping persons to love themselves and be more comfortable with and accepting of themselves.

The program also supports and encourages participation in the "Beginning Experience Weekend." This is a program designed to close the door on the past and to help one start over again. This program is based in the Roman Catholic Church and is open to persons of all faiths. It is offered in many parts of the country and world.

The Coplens summarize their purpose: "Our greatest goal is to win these hurting people back to Christ."

Resources and References

Ahrons, Constance. 1983. "Divorce: Before, During, and After," in *Stress and the Family,* vol. 1, *Coping with Normative Transitions,* ed. Hamilton I. McCubbin and Charles R. Figley (New York: Brunner/Mazel), pp. 102–115.

Alan Guttmacher Institute. 1976. *11 Million Teenagers: What Can Be Done About the Epidemic of Adolescent Pregnancies in the United States.* New York: Planned Parenthood Federation of America.

Baptist Leader. 1983. Vol. 45, no. 1 (April).

Blume, Judy. 1972. *It's Not the End of the World.* Scarsdale, N.Y.: Bradbury Press.

Brown, Raymond K. 1979. *Reach Out to Singles: A Challenge to Ministry.* Philadelphia: Westminster Press.

Burgess-Kohn, Jane, and Willard K. Kohn. 1979. *The Widower.* Boston: Beacon Press.

Bustanoby, Andre. 1985. *Being a Single Parent.* Grand Rapids: Zondervan Publishing House.

Caine, Lynn. 1974. *Widow.* New York: Bantam Books.

Carter, Velma Thorne, and J. Lynn Leavenworth. 1985. *Caught in the Middle: The Children of Divorce.* Valley Forge, Pa.: Judson Press.

————. 1977. *Putting the Pieces Together: Help for Single Parents.* Valley Forge, Pa.: Judson Press.

Christoff, Nicholas. 1980. *Saturday Night, Sunday Morning: Singles and the Church.* New York: Harper & Row.

Claussen, Russell, ed. 1980. *The Church's Growing Edge: Single Adults.* New York: Pilgrim Press.

Dalke, David. 1977. "A Model of Ministry to the Divorce-Caused Single Parent Family." Unpublished dissertation for the Doctor of Ministry, San Francisco Theological Seminary.

————. Undated. *The Healing Divorce: A Practical and Theological Approach.* Longmont, Colo.: Learnings Unlimited.

Detrich, Richard L., and Nicola J. Steele. 1983. *How to Recover from Grief.* Valley Forge, Pa.: Judson Press.

Etzler, Carole. 1980. *Single.* Joint Educational Development. A three-minute motion picture on the struggle of singles for acceptance in the church. Available from American Baptist Films (Valley Forge, PA 19481, or Box 23204, Oakland, CA 94623).

Family Relations (Journal of Applied Family and Child Studies). 1986. Special issue on the single-parent family, vol. 35, no. 1 (January).

Fisher, Bruce. 1981. *Rebuilding: When Your Relationship Ends.* San Luis Obispo, Calif.: Impact Publishers.

Gardner, Richard A. 1978. *The Boys' and Girls' Book About Divorce.* New York: G. P. Putnam's Sons.

Gladow, Nancy Wells, and Margaret P. Ray. 1986. "The Impact of Information Support Systems on the Well-being of Low-Income Single Parents." *Family Relations*, vol. 35, no. 1 (January), pp. 113–123.

Hanson, Shirley M. H., and Michael J. Sporakowski. 1986. "Single Parent Families." *Family Relations*, vol. 35, no. 1 (January), pp. 3–8.

Hazen, Barbara Shook. 1978. *Two Homes to Live In: A Child's Eye View of Divorce.* New York: Human Sciences Press.

Hogan, M. Janice, Cheryl Buehler, and Beatrice Robinson. 1983. "Single Parenting: Transitioning Alone." In Hamilton McCubbin and Charles R. Figley, eds., *Stress and the Family*, vol. 1. New York: Brunner/Mazel.

Johnson, Douglas W. 1982. *The Challenge of Single Adult Ministry.* Valley Forge, Pa.: Judson Press.

Johnson, Nancy K. 1982. *Alone and Beginning Again.* Valley Forge, Pa.: Judson Press.

Krantzler, Mel. 1975. *Creative Divorce.* New York: New American Library, Signet Books.

————. 1977. *Learning to Love Again: Beyond Creative Divorce.* New York: Thomas Y. Crowell.

Kreis, Bernadine, and Alice Pattie. 1969. *Up from Grief: Patterns of Recovery.* New York: Seabury Press.

Lewis, C. S. 1976. *A Grief Observed.* New York: Bantam Books.

Lindsay, Rae. 1981. "Alone and Surviving: The Two Million Widows Under 55," *Theos Magazine,* vol. 20, no. 5 (May), pp. 3–5.

Loewinsohn, Ruth Jean. 1979. *Survival Handbook for Widows.* Chicago: Follett Publishing Co.

Morgan, Richard Lyon. 1985. *Is There Life After Divorce in the Church?* Atlanta: John Knox Press.

Murdock, Carol. 1980. *Single Parents Are People Too.* Altoona, Pa.: Butterick Publishing.

Oates, Wayne E. 1976. *Pastoral Care and Counseling in Grief and Separation.* Philadelphia: Fortress Press.

Paylor, Neil, and Perry Head. 1983. *Scenes from a Divorce: A Book for Relatives and Friends of the Divorcing Family.* Minneapolis: Winston Press.

Powell, John S., and Loretta Brady. 1980. "Fully Alive Experience." Audiotape. Allen, Tex.: Tabor Publishing Co. Guidebook from Argus.

Richards, Sue Poorman, and Stanley Hagemeyer. 1986. *Ministering to the Divorced: Guidance, Structure, and Organization That Promote Healing in the Church.* Grand Rapids: Zondervan Publishing House.

Risman, Barbara J. 1986. "Can Men 'Mother'? Life as a Single Father." *Family Relations,* vol. 35, no. 1 (January), pp. 95–102.

Silverman, Phyllis, et al. 1974. *Helping Each Other in Widowhood.* New York: Health Sciences Publishing Corp.

Spilke, Francine S. 1979. *The Family That Changed: A Child's Book About Divorce.* New York: Crown Publishers.

Stewart, Suzanne. 1978. *Parent Alone.* Waco, Tex.: Word Books.

U.S. Bureau of the Census. 1988. *Fertility of American Women: June 1987.* Current Population Reports, Series P-20, no. 427. Washington, D.C.: U.S. Government Printing Office.

Weiss, Robert S. 1979. *Going It Alone: The Family Life and Social Situation of the Single Parent.* New York: Basic Books.

4

Images of Remarried Families

Remarriage has become an important new reality of family life in the late twentieth century. The sheer number of such families compels our attention. The complicated dynamics of the blended family units that result where there are children deserve sensitive pastoral care and support.

Of all marriages now being contracted, 46 percent include at least one person who was previously married. In 1970 the comparable figure was only 30 percent (U.S. Bureau of the Census 1987, p. 83). Frank Furstenberg notes, "Given present levels of remarriage—about three fourths of all females and five sixths of all males reenter marriage after divorce—it seems likely that no less than a fourth of all adults will have wed more than once by midlife" (Furstenberg 1980, p. 444). If the rate of divorce does not decline, the probability that an individual will live in a remarried family either while growing up or as an adult is close to, if not greater than, one in two (ibid.). It is estimated there are fifteen million stepchildren under the age of eighteen. One observer notes that 35 percent of all children in America will live some part of their lives in a stepfamily (Sukosky 1985, p. 14).

Remarriage today is different from remarriage in the past. Throughout history there have been numbers of remarriages, but until this century almost all remarriages followed widowhood. For example, in the Plymouth Colony about one third of all men and one fourth of all women who lived full lifetimes after the death of a spouse remarried There was little divorce in that colony. Even as late as the 1920s, in the United States, more remarriages occurred among widowed people than among the divorced (Cherlin 1978, p. 637). But by 1984, at least three fourths of all remarrying brides and remarrying grooms had been previously divorced (U.S. Department of Health and Human Services 1988, Table 1–28). The existence of living ex-spouses is a relatively new factor in remarriages.

The statistics on the fragility of remarriages are equally staggering. One pair of observers notes that the divorce rate is 30 to 40 percent for first marriages, 60 percent for second marriages, 80 percent for third marriages, and 90 percent for fourth marriages (Houmes and Meier 1985). Other estimates are a bit more optimistic, but all would admit that those observations are not far off the mark. Yet another pair notes that 40 percent of all second marriages end in divorce within four years! (Visher and Visher 1980, p. xix). Persons in remarriages face a most difficult task, and particularly so in the early years of that remarriage.

Such information may be hard to believe for the faithful church leader. Perhaps one does not note anywhere nearly that proportion of divorces and remarriages among the members of one's congregation. There might be several reasons for this. Persons often drop out of sight when marital breakup occurs. They may go to a different church or to none. If so, they may lose the support of the church family through that difficult time. People who join a church may well not publicize the fact that they are a remarried family because of the stigma of divorce and the fear of rejection. Many remarried families are entirely churchless. They may not believe that any church has a place for them or anything to offer them.

Metaphors for Remarried Families

What is the situation for remarried families? We will attempt to describe it by using a series of images. These images are not meant to demean persons or remarriage. We have the highest respect for those couples who have persisted to make their remarriages happy and enduring unions—they are among the pioneers of our society, and we have much to learn from them. Rather, these images suggest complex tasks for remarrieds and note that support for these families is often inadequate.

A Shaky Building with Some of the Pillars Missing

Remarried families are deprived of some very important supports: a language to talk about themselves; legal precedents; parenting patterns; and supportive societal norms.

In noting this fact, one sociologist, Andrew Cherlin, calls remarriage an "incomplete institution" (1978, pp. 634–650). By institution, the sociologist means those enduring, predictable, habitual, reliable behaviors that exist in a relationship. (One's social setting teaches and reinforces these behaviors, until everyone "knows" how you are supposed to act.) For example, we all know what a mother is and what a father is, and how they are supposed to behave, with what authority and power. While there are variations, the roles are quite clearly defined in our society. The presence of such habitualized patterns contributes to family unity. The most important psychological gain is that the family has fewer decisions to face. By routinizing everyday life in family living, there will be fewer points at which the family must struggle over how to conduct family life (Cherlin 1978, p. 636).

In the remarried family, this habitualization of family life is often absent—particularly in the early years of a remarriage. And when the patterns are established, the family has had to struggle for much of this themselves. This family type has had little help from the society in which its members live.

There are several areas in which this phenomenon makes remarriages more difficult. One area is language. At first thought, this might seem fairly minor. However, when no adequate terms exist for such important roles as stepfather, stepmother, or stepchild, there is both confusion and lack of societal support (Cherlin 1978, p. 643). We do indeed lack adequate, universally accepted language. We don't know what to call this family unit. The term "stepparent" (literally, grief parent) originally meant a parent who replaced a dead one, not a parent stepping into a partial role also occupied by a divorced parent. The term step- carried negative connotations. There is no widespread agreement on alternate terms for the unit, such as "blended family." There are no adequate terms for what children should call their parents' new spouses. With vagueness in terms, there is also vagueness in rights and duties of members of this new family unit.

Another area of difficulty is that of law. Implicit in law is the assumption that the marriage in question is a first marriage. Quite commonly in most states, there is no provision for several problems of remarriage. Issues needing attention include balancing financial obligations of husbands to their spouses and children from current and from previous marriages, and defining the wife's obligations to husbands and children from new and from old marriages. When a death occurs, there is little legal guidance for reconciling the competing claims of current and former spouses for rights to a portion of the estate. Legal regulations concerning incest and consanguineous marriage need to be redefined for families of remarriage (Cherlin 1978, p. 644).

Still other vaguely defined areas include the proper disciplinary relationship of a new spouse to the partner's children. How should parenthood be shared in the new household? And how should one relate to one's former spouse and former in-laws, including the grand-parents of one's children? What is the proper etiquette, or courtesy, for treating one's former spouse when he or she comes to pick up or return the children? Is such a person invited in? offered drink or food? treated on a social basis? And what about that ex-spouse's family network? One sociologist calls these people "quasi kin." What contact should be maintained? Should they be involved in major events in the lives of the children?

The incompleteness of the institution of remarriage is at least one factor in contributing to the tremendously vague, uncertain feeling that clouds many early remarriages. Persons have expressed this feeling in some vivid metaphors. Becoming a stepparent in a remar-riage is like "trying to follow an unfamiliar path in the dark. . . . The path seems lonely even though there are millions of others walking down the same trail" (Visher and Visher 1982, p. 2). It is like trying to learn to swim by jumping in the deep end, rather than the shallow end, of the pool; parachuting into an unknown territory and being expected to perform effectively, even when you don't know the language, the customs, or the rules; or stepping into a play already in progress—you know that somehow you are involved, but you don't know the plot, you don't know who all the cast members are (and there are many), and nobody seems to give you a script for your part! (Olson and Della Pia–Terry, 1984a, p. 64).

The institutional supports of which we speak emerge slowly in a society. For the foreseeable future, remarried families themselves will need to struggle with much too wide a range of decision-making. They will need to build their own expectations, rituals, habits, and customs as a family.

Wheels Within a Wheel

There are still other ways to look at the new stepfamily. One might be as "wheels within a wheel." We are not referring to Ezekiel's vision or the delightful spiritual we sing to celebrate that. Rather, we speak of one large circle or "wheel"—the new, remarried family—and of the many little "wheels" within that larger one. This understanding comes from Family Systems Theory. Practitioners of that discipline speak of the family "system" and the "subsystems" within. We will appropriate their insights using our own metaphor. Jamie Kelem Keshet identifies several "wheels" (subsystems) within the stepfamily (1980, pp. 520–524).

First is the ex-spouse wheel, which once included many bonds (residence, mutual conversations, sexual relations, coparenting, for example). By the time of divorce this has become a relationship that is "held together primarily by past history, legal and financial obligations, and a common commitment to child-rearing."

Second is the parent-child wheel, which includes both the resident and the nonresident parent. The residential parent-child wheel may have grown very strong as children live with the fears of losing a remaining parent. The remaining parent may also cling more closely to the child. In later, more stable stages, this grouping may have become a self-sufficient unit with a strong outer boundary. This may well be a unit very difficult to integrate into a stepfamily. Its members may not be eager to share their newfound intimacy and equality with new people. Visiting parent-child wheels, on the other hand, will vary widely in their effectiveness and cohesiveness.

The new-remarried-couple wheel is the newest subgroup and is often the most fragile. This relationship may initially form somewhat apart from the other partner's children. In this courtship period, a bond is formed and the decision to marry is made. Thus, a fledgling couple relationship finds itself encountering and engaging several sturdy, long-standing "wheels" as they attempt to combine into a functioning stepfamily unit.

As Keshet notes, the new stepfamily system threatens each of these relational units, and they in turn threaten the new stepfamily. At the same time, there is also a possibility that the interrelationship can be one of mutual strengthening.

The remarriage can affect the ex-spouse relationship both negatively and positively. It may enable the ex-spouses to recognize and do the work of separating emotionally. But it may also make cooperation as postdivorce parents of the same children even more difficult.

The stepfamily interacts with the parent-child "wheel" by challenging the tightly closed circle. This new family asks for admittance of another person or persons. At the same time it can relieve children of responsibility for the parent's emotional well-being, and perhaps for some practical household tasks. This may in turn free the child for more autonomy, and for more energy for relationships with peers and with siblings. The new adult (stepparent) may be very slowly admitted as a resource adult. The new couple may find their relationship threatened by their large responsibilities and by conflicts over appropriate involvement in the various relationships whirling around them. On the other hand, a shared life both with a spouse and with one's children can be a strong source of satisfaction.

Keshet notes it is quite logical that these various groupings will compete for scarce resources such as time and finances and that the negotiating of these needs can be a beneficial process. She points out that some stepfamily members will hold membership in more than one of these "wheels." These persons are the pivotal persons in resolving their conflicting needs.

After Keshet has analyzed the stepfamily she draws these hopeful conclusions (1980, pp. 530–531).

> The individual members and subunits of a stepfamily can, however, learn together to reach common goals and to enjoy common satisfactions. The development of this unity within the stepfamily is facilitated by (1) resolution of conflicts within the subsystems, (2) negotiations between subsystems for fulfillment of competing needs and distribution of resources, (3) weakening of boundaries between subsystems, (4) recognition that the stepfamily cannot duplicate the nuclear family model and (5) a strong fulfilling couple relationship which enables the partners to cope with the complications of the stepfamily.

A Crowded Vehicle

In a vivid paragraph, Morton Hunt has written, "Unlike the young who come to each other relatively empty handed, the divorced (or widowed) man and divorced (or widowed) woman come with all the acquisitions of the years—their individual histories, habits, and tastes, their children, friends, and chattels. Love can be a rickety vehicle, loaded with much of life's baggage" (Hunt 1966, p. 269).

We might add that this vehicle of which Hunt speaks is often extremely crowded. For example, consider the experience of a friend and sometime writing partner who went into a bank and said to an official, "I'm Carole Della Pia–Terry, and I'd like to open a new account here." The official responded, "That sounds more like a corporation than a person!" As Carole reflected, "He was much more accurate than he knew. There are thirty-one people who, so to speak, own a piece of me. And those are just the main ones. There are many more persons in this family structure."

Or as another man put it, "I didn't marry my wife, I married a crowd. . . . There are my three sons who give me the silent treatment when they see me every other weekend, *and* the twin ten-year-old daughters of my new wife Carolyn, who frankly are often a pain . . . *and* my new in-laws, who cold-shoulder me, *and* Carolyn's ex-husband, who spoils the kids rotten when he sees them, *and* my ex-wife, who is still bad-mouthing me to my kids, *and* the Bank of America's Credit and Loan Department" (Krantzler 1977, p. 219).

Those persons have put it well. Remarriage can well be a crowded and rickety vehicle.

Overabundance of Family Legacies

Furthermore, a remarried family will have many past experiences—family legacies, if you will—that shape their ideas of what a family is and how it should function.

For example, consider the new family of Phoebe and Rick. Phoebe was married seven years and had two children before she divorced. After three years of being a single parent she married Rick, a widower who had one son and who had functioned with him as a single parent. When these folks began their new family life together, at least six different family heritages influenced the family's decisions:

1. The family in which Phoebe grew up
2. Phoebe's first-marriage family
3. The single-parent family of Phoebe and her two children
4. The family in which Rick grew up
5. Rick's first-marriage family
6. The single-parent family of Rick and his son

When this family comes together and begins its life, there may be at least six opinions about "when to go to bed, where to put the television, how to light a fire, bake cookies, make pancakes, drive a car, and celebrate holidays" (Visher and Visher 1982, pp. 7–8).

A Multidirectional Tug-of-War

Persons who enter a remarriage frequently speak of experiencing a good bit of strain, particularly in the early years. Members of the new unit sense that they are pulling against a number of resistances to bring this new family experience into being. Virtually all members of the new remarried family will feel this. But the question is, Who are the pullers, and who are the pulled, and in what direction are persons pulling?

The new stepparent may see the spouse's children as the resisters. And these children may well feel a prime loyalty to their biological parents and to the first marriage. Some stepparents may suspect that children are attempting to sabotage the new marriage so that original parents can get back together. Children may feel it is disloyal to biological parents to express love and acceptance of stepparents, likable though those stepparents may be. Further, children may be socialized to trust biological parents and distrust other adults. The newly remarried couple may sense that they are pulling in the direction of family unity. They may feel that the children of either or both spouses are the pullers against such unity.

The children, however, may feel more like the pulled. Sometimes they may even feel like the tug rope between unaccepting ex-spouses.

At other times they may find themselves confused by their changed place in the family, both in regard to parents and in regard to siblings and stepsiblings. (For instance, a child who once was the youngest may, in the restructured family, have become a middle child.)

At the same time, the whole family is pulling against unrealistically high expectations. Family members may have a hard time sorting out normal family stresses from those special to the remarried family. Sometimes they are also contending with the normal problems of building a new family unit.

Patience and communication are the keys to arriving at the discovery that they are all on the same side. When that happens, the new family is born.

A Revolving Door and a Revolving Charge Account

One symbol of the remarried family is the revolving door. For the resident membership of such a family does not remain constant.

Many family courts are moving in the direction of granting joint custody of children to divorcing parents. For some children this means spending almost equal time in each of two parents' homes—parents who no longer live together. For others it means going from one parent's home to the other for shorter stays. It might be school week in one home, weekends in the other; school year in one home, summers in the other; or part of vacations, weekends, and holidays in one home and part in the other.

If each remarried partner brings children from a previous marriage, their home may sometimes shelter children from both marriages, or from either of the previous marriages. Each combination has its possibilities for relating, cooperating, and competing.

All family members may have problems with entry and exit when the members of the family scene change constantly. All will need to learn to deal with loneliness when someone leaves and discomfort when someone reenters.

Remarried families need to develop special skills and styles to let the occasional family members know that they have a place. Those who come and go need to know that they belong, whether present or absent. The families need to learn how to let children go and welcome them back.

But along with the symbol of the revolving door, an equally appropriate one might be the revolving charge account. For as children come and go within the remarriage, so does money. A stepfather might have financial obligations for the raising of his biological children who live elsewhere. A mother might be receiving child-support payments from an ex-husband. In each case, financial decisions need to be faced: How do we handle the costs for this medical or dental need of a child? What about music, instruments, increased education or cultural opportunities? What about inflation and the increased expenses of growing children? There are many decisions that will need to be made about how much money should stay, how much money should come in, and how much money should go out. These decisions also involve negotiating with a wide number of people.

The Shake-and-Bake Family

Dan Houmes and Paul Meier (1985, pp. 103–114) describe Bill and Mary, who met in a grocery store and quickly discovered a commonality of faith, family situation (divorce), and loneliness. After a ten-month whirlwind romance, they married and Bill moved into Mary's house with her three extremely active children, ages sixteen, fourteen, and twelve. In addition, Bill's son and daughter occasionally came for visits of several days.

Very early in the marriage, Mary's children's needs seemed to grow and Mary became ever more involved with them. While Bill felt a vague discontent about this, work demands were claiming extra time from him as well. Much too quickly, the joy and satisfaction they had felt in their earlier courtship was dissipating.

Houmes and Meier call this the "Shake-and-Bake" family—that is, the instant family. It suffered from

Too little time, and no time at all as a couple before children were present
Too little bonding between stepparents and children, so the stepparent may be tempted gradually to withdraw
Too many responsibilities—work, time, financial, parenting, kin, marriage
Too many complications, such as reconciling conflicting needs and schedules
Too few adjustments

Every marriage needs time for adjustment, recommitment, and stabilizing. And yet the instant demands placed on the remarrying couple may render time to do that difficult or impossible.

There is need for skill in negotiating the scarce resources of a remarriage so the couple may find strength to make it go. Such families might well benefit from expressions of support—such as offers to take the kids for a weekend or an afternoon.

A Temple

Tom and Adrienne Frydenger offer a beautiful image of the stepfamily drawing close together in bonding. They first recall the baby that was born to their union and the bonding that occurred during the time of the pregnancy, the birth, and immediately after birth. Quite naturally, this led to shared experiences with their new baby. They ask,

If an adult comes into children's lives later as a stepparent, how can some bonding take place? They suggest the image of Solomon's Temple, with its three different areas.

First there was the outer court, bustling with activities. They suggest that just as anyone could enter the outer court, so anyone can enter into activities with children. These activities are a safe place for bonding to begin between stepparent and stepchild. This should be initiated by the stepparent and should center on the child's interests. The purpose is to provide opportunities for the child to have fun and to associate those good times with the stepparent.

Then there was the holy place. This implies bonding through the exchange of ideas. And just as a sign above the holy place might have read PRIESTS ONLY, NO ONE ELSE ALLOWED, so the sign posted between a child's activities and that child's thoughts and feelings might say, FRIENDS ONLY. UNCARING PEOPLE STAY OUT. Faithfulness in shared activities may occasionally allow the stepparent entrance into this part of the child's life. The goal of bonding through the exchange of ideas is not to lecture. It is rather to hear what is going on in the child's life.

Last there was the Holy of Holies, and this implies bonding at its deepest level. The Frydengers note that the Old Testament priests entered the Holy of Holies only once a year, for the Day of Atonement. The stepparent, if fortunate, may have about the same number of chances to enter into spiritual bonding with the child. They suggest that since these opportunities are so infrequent, it is important to use them sensitively and well. They suggest (1984, pp. 113–114):

> Walk in softly, slowly, and follow your stepchild's leading.
> Be sensitive and realize that the situation and the child's feelings are important.
> Be available. Though it may sound simple, being available is one of the biggest commitments you can make. You can judge your availability by your willingness to put down the paper, to go shopping, or turn off the football game when your attention is needed. . . .
> Be sure your motivation for helping is pure. . . .
> Be secure in yourself. Don't feel angry or threatened when your stepchild talks to you about your spouse's ex-mate.

With such sensitivities, the Frydengers suggest, the stepparent may be admitted into the Holy of Holies of an occasional spiritual bonding with a stepchild.

In Summary

The Vishers have summarized what we have said by noting five structural characteristics of remarried families in which they differ from the first-marriage nuclear family: (1) Virtually all members of these new families have sustained the loss of a primary relationship; (2) where the remarriage was preceded by a divorce, one biological parent probably lives outside the current family unit; (3) the relationship between the adult couple in the household is predated by the relationship of parents to biological children; (4) role definitions are weak; and (5) usually the children in remarried households have membership in more than one household (Visher and Visher 1979).

Remarried families face an extremely complex set of tasks that must be accomplished if they are to succeed as an enduring and satisfying family unit. The difficulty of their tasks will vary widely from family to family. Circumstances that reduce the complexity are: having only one spouse with a previous marriage; having children from only one member of the new couple; children being younger, rather than older, at the time of the second marriage; and the children and other extended family members viewing the new union with enthusiasm. But virtually every remarried family will face some struggle in adjustment.

A Theological Response

Our theology of family propels us into ministry with remarried units.

In most remarriages, there are persons who are recovering from broken covenants. Some may have left an earlier covenant too easily. Others have been abandoned. Many persons may have been damaged or hurt in those earlier relationships. But the God of forgiveness, rebirth, and resurrection can bless the new union and lead persons to new covenants. These new covenants should be made solemnly and realistically with an understanding of how much effort will be needed to live out these promises. Those who enter into this new marriage covenant need to be aware there will undoubtedly be resistances, but resistances can be overcome. There will be barriers, but walls can be dismantled. There may be alienation, but alienated persons can be reconciled.

We believe that when persons enter a remarriage, they are undertaking a type of marriage and family covenant that may be even more difficult to maintain than a first marriage, because of its many ill-defined and complex roles. But we also believe that a remarriage can be blessed and is worthy of skilled pastoral care and support from the whole church community.

Appropriate Care

What can church leaders offer remarrying families?
Caring ministers can reach a decision that they will minister to

remarried families (and their first issue is often deciding to preside over weddings where one or both are remarrying). They can further decide that they will do it energetically with all the skill and insight they can muster.

Churches also need to wrestle with this issue. Clergy and their churches are sometimes far apart in this matter. As a result, too often while the minister tries to include remarried families, other church persons sabotage those efforts. Since churches consist of many individuals, such a decision of the clergy will never carry over to every member. Still, a frank discussion with policy-making boards of acceptance of changing families, including remarried families, is much in order.

As part of this clarifying effort, ministers should discover if their denomination has a policy about remarriages and ministry with remarried families.

A minister can then offer helpful premarriage counseling to those who come to him or her to be married. The minister will quickly discover that most prepared resources for premarriage counseling simply do not fit the remarrying couple. A book that can help ministers in premarriage counseling with remarrying persons is *Ministry with Remarried Persons* (Olson and Della Pia–Terry 1984b). It suggests that the issues are: Has each of you sufficiently recovered from the pain of past losses to be ready for this commitment? What is your explicit marital contract with each other and what is as yet unknown? What is the state of your couple relationship, and what plans do you have to keep nurturing it? How are the children and other involved people responding to these plans? If there are resistances, how are you dealing with them? Where are you in your decisions on parenting, discipline, family structure, family housing, and family finance? How do you feel about conflict, and have you begun to work out a conflict-management style? How are you doing theologically and in regard to plans for faith, ritual, and church participation in your emerging stepfamily? (Olson and Della Pia–Terry 1984b, pp. 31–53).

Churches can learn to be sensitive to the remarried family's situation. For example, they can call people by their right names. (There may be two or more surnames in a remarried household, and people want to be called by their proper names.) Church groups can be sensitive to the complicated schedules in the lives of children in such families. These children may be gone on a regular basis (every other weekend, or all summer, for example) to another parent's household. There can be some effort to fit exciting church events into the children's schedules—as far as possible. Teachers may be able to design each church school class activity as complete in itself. If that is not possible, a caring teacher can help a child keep abreast of what is happening in church school during these necessary absences. What we suggest may not be realistic in large churches with numerous children from remarried families. Still, heightened sensitivity and caring may be necessary, lest valuable children feel left out and as a result drop out of the class.

Churches can be sensitive to stepparents and see them as part of the parental team concerned about a child's learning, growth, and all-around development. (They are not always treated so in many communities.) The church that cares for remarried families communicates, "We accept you and enter into partnership with you in the personal spiritual growth of each member of your family. We desire the spiritual strengthening of your entire family unit."

Perhaps the remarried couples might like to experience support from others in their same circumstances. This could take a one-couple-to-one-couple form of support. Or it might be a group (either for social purposes or family growth purposes, or both) of remarried couples. Children of remarriage might at times appreciate such a sharing group as well.

Pastoral leaders should be sensitized to signs of family distress in all types of family. The clergyperson will want to be informed as to the best family-treatment resources—with sensitivity to remarried families—and sometimes intervene to make a referral.

How Some Churches Have Ministered

Ministers and churches have responded to the needs of remarried couples on at least two levels. First there is the level of pastoral care— pastors respond to an individual couple or family. Then there is the level of programs. Some congregations minister to remarried families in groups.

An example of the first level comes from Rhode Island. A minister there has found ways to respond individually to remarrying couples that come to him. For one thing, he tailors the premarriage preparation to their needs. He uses the Prepare/Enrich marriage counseling material, which has separate material for families involved in remarriage. When planning the wedding ceremony, he urges the couple to involve the children as much as seems appropriate for their situation. For example, in one of the wedding services, the minister asked the children of a previous marriage, "Will you pledge to continue your love for them [their mother and new stepfather], and to work together with them for the future of your lives together?" The children's response was "We will." Often the pastoral prayer at a wedding includes the children of the remarriage as well. Through both premarriage counseling and the wedding ceremony itself celebrating the new union, this minister acknowledges and encourages the entire family unit.

An example of the second level of response comes from the Downtown Cooperative Parish of Racine, Wisconsin. It sponsored a short course for persons concerned about remarriage. This parish is a coalition of nine Protestant and Catholic churches.

The modest expenses for the course were funded equally by all the churches. Some of the churches promoted it actively, some very passively. With a good bit of upbeat publicity, approximately twenty-five persons participated in the event. Of these, approximately one fourth were professionals in counseling who felt the need for more awareness of remarriage. While planners had hoped for a larger response, they later learned that this was a remarkably good attendance. For whatever reasons, sessions for remarried folks are often poorly attended. They learned also that they were wiser than they realized in making their publicity upbeat and positive. Participants told them that this approach gave those who felt hesitant encouragement to at least try out the event.

This group met four times. For the first two sessions, an outstanding family sociologist and an excellent couple therapist team—themselves remarried—made presentations and carried on dialogue with the group. A third session was given over to conflict in the remarried family, and a fourth was devoted to parenting and discipline issues.

The participants were amazed at the amount of closeness and sharing that emerged in so short a time. Several had enthusiasm for an ongoing support group. Unfortunately, both founders were transferred from the community at about that time, so the support group was not called into being. The leaders also discovered that some persons came to the group too troubled to be helped in such a setting. And so they had to use their counseling skills privately and make referrals for such persons. The fact that it was sponsored by a group of churches seemed to make it easier for some to come. All in all, leaders and participants felt that it was a good and helpful experience. Such an effort was a statement from some churches to remarried persons that their family form was worthy of attention and support. This message was heard and appreciated even by remarried persons who chose not to participate in the event.

A much more elaborate ministry with remarried persons has been developed at the First Presbyterian Church of Colorado Springs, Colorado. This is a large church with a powerful ministry among singles entitled "Going Concern." This program had many facets, including a Sunday morning class that had 250 in attendance on a typical Sunday. Predictably, many marriages occurred between persons in this group. The remarried persons, however, experienced a vacuum in church activities appropriate to them. No longer did they fit in the singles ministry. On the other hand, some did not feel particularly comfortable in the established couples classes either.

One evening four couples, all previously members of the singles ministry, met together socially. At the end of the evening, a conversation about remarriage began. This was found to be not only unthreatening, but welcome. They vowed to meet again. And they did so, this time with six couples in attendance. Sensing a need for human and divine support for their marriages, the couples founded an organization that included social events and study groups. One group explored Christian marriage in general, and another explored the resource book *Help for Remarried Couples and Families* (Olson and Della Pia–Terry 1984a). By now, there were twenty couples on the roster.

The effort had developed this far quite spontaneously. At this point, some of the leaders sought church support and recognition, including a Sunday church school class specifically for remarried folks. Marcia and Pete Peterson, two of the cofounders, informed their pastor of what had transpired. They recall, "He was not only accepting but enthusiastic about our embryonic efforts. He also knew that if the group was to survive and prosper, to reach its full potential in helping the Lord to work in each of us, the group must come under the umbrella of the church."

Though there were some delays due to pastoral staff changes, the Sunday morning class did come into being. The executive minister of the congregation became the teacher. It was decided that remarried couples and those contemplating remarriage who had begun the premarital interview process with the pastor would be welcome. The following is a description by the Petersons of their Sunday morning experience:

> The class meets every Sunday from 9:20 to 10:30 A.M. We spend the first ten to fifteen minutes in what we could call "coffee table fellowship" and (important!) greeting new members and visitors. Singing begins about 9:30 and hopefully all find a place to sit. There follow the usual business and announcements which we try to hold to a *minimum*. Ideally that leaves from 9:45 until 10 to have one couple share something about marriage that they might have learned by study or by experience. This is probably the part of the class that is unique. Rev. Smith follows at 10 with a prepared lesson of about thirty minutes. He has been successful in illustrating the challenge of remarriage with biblical references.

The group continues to sponsor social events such as retreats, small group dinners, and specific study groups.

The Petersons ask, "Where do we go from here? . . . We hope to grow in our marriages and knowledge of Christ's love for us. We hope to expand our influence in the community. . . . We will let the Lord decide on our role over the years."

Resources and References

Burns, Cherie. 1986. *Stepmotherhood: How to Survive Without Feeling Frustrated, Left Out, or Wicked.* New York: Harper & Row.

Capaldi, Fredrick, and Barbara McRae. 1979. *Stepfamilies: A Cooperative Responsibility.* New York: Franklin Watts.

Cherlin, Andrew. 1978. "Remarriage as an Incomplete Institution." *American Journal of Sociology*, vol. 84, no. 3, pp. 634–650.

Frydenger, Tom, and Adrienne Frydenger. 1984. *The Blended Family.* Grand Rapids: Zondervan Publishing House.

Furstenberg, Frank F., Jr. 1980. "Reflections on Remarriage." *Journal of Family Issues*, vol. 1, no. 4 (December), pp. 443–453.

Gorman, Tony. 1983. *Stepfather.* Boulder, Colo.: Gentle Touch Press.

Houmes, Dan, and Paul Meier. 1985. *Growing in Step.* Richardson, Tex.: Today Publishers.

Humphrey, Penny. 1987. *Stepmothers Try Harder.* New York: Henry Holt & Co.

Hunt, Morton M. 1966. *The World of the Formerly Married.* New York: McGraw-Hill Book Co.

Keshet, Jamie Kelem. 1980. "From Separation to Stepfamily: A Subsystem Analysis." *Journal of Family Issues*, vol. 1, no. 4 (December), pp. 517–532.

————. 1986. *Love and Power in the Stepfamily.* New York: McGraw-Hill Book Co.

Krantzler, Mel. 1977. *Learning to Love Again: Beyond Creative Divorce.* New York: Thomas Y. Crowell.

Messinger, Lillian. 1984. *Remarriage: A Family Affair.* New York: Plenum Publishing Corp.

Olson, Richard P., and Carole Della Pia–Terry. 1984a. *Help for Remarried Couples and Families.* Valley Forge, Pa.: Judson Press.

————. 1984b. *Ministry with Remarried Persons.* Valley Forge, Pa.: Judson Press. This work also contains a more extensive bibliography and a six-session program guide.

Prepare/Enrich. P.O. Box 190, Minneapolis, MN 55458-0190.

Sager, Clifford J., et al. 1983. *Treating the Remarried Family.* New York: Brunner/Mazel.

Stuart, Richard B., and Barbara Jacobson. 1985. *Second Marriage: Make It Happy! Make It Last!* New York: W. W. Norton & Co.

Sukosky, Donald G. 1985. "Making the Most of Blended Families." *Family Life Educator*, vol. 4, no. 2 (Winter), pp. 14–17.

U.S. Bureau of the Census. 1987. *Statistical Abstract of the United States: 1988* (108th ed.). Washington, D.C.: U.S. Government Printing Office.

U.S. Department of Health and Human Services. National Center for Health Statistics. 1988. *Vital Statistics of the United States,* 1984, vol. 3, Marriage and Divorce. DHHS pub. no. (PHS) 88–1103 (Public Health Service). Washington, D.C.: U.S. Government Printing Office.

Visher, Emily B., and John S. Visher. 1979. *Stepfamilies: A Guide to Working with Stepparents and Stepchildren*. New York: Brunner/Mazel.

_____. 1980. *A Stepfamily Workshop Manual*. Stepfamily Association of California.

_____. 1982. *How to Win as a Stepfamily*. New York: Dembner Books.

5

Religious or
Value Differences

Visualize your neighborhood on a Sunday morning. There are the families that leave for church together in one car, and there are those who leave in two cars for different churches. In some homes, part of the family goes and some stay home. Perhaps parents attend worship and the children do not. Or one parent and some children do. In some instances children have found a new church different from that of their heritage, and they attend while parents do not.

Not so easily observed is the variety of sexual norms and behaviors with which the families on this street are involved. Like parents in previous generations, many parents are concerned about their children's sexual behavior. What has changed is that parents and children may not be operating from the same sexual values. One mother is struggling over whether to discuss birth control with her subteen daughter, and whether to help her obtain information on birth control methods. Parents of another girl live with the difficulty of responding to a teenage pregnancy. Yet another family is wrestling with what will be appropriate arrangements when their son brings home the woman with whom he is living. And another is struggling with feelings about themselves and their son who has just written his parents that he is gay.

Myriad other religious and value issues are dealt with within each family on this street almost daily. Attitudes toward education, persons in authority, employment, money, saving, and standard of living vary within a family and occasion arguments. The values expressed in videos, music, and movies may arouse more conflict.

It would seem that the answer to the question, How many families have religious and value differences? is: All of them! Some of these conflicts, however, are more frequent, and some are more severe. We will give brief attention to several of these.

Religious Differences

Differences in Belief, Practice, and Participation

One of us—Joe—conducts workshops on the church's role in strengthening family life. The question most frequently encountered at these is, "How can we be of help to the family where only one spouse participates in the life of the church?"

This difference in faith and church involvement has several possible sources. The nonparticipating person may simply have grown up in a home that had no, or minimal, participation in church life. Or she or he may have had an unfortunate experience with a church. Some conflict, criticism, failure by a church leader (or the church) to live out its faith might have led to disillusionment and withdrawal.

Another contributing factor in the number of families with religious differences is a growing privatism and individualism about religion (among other things) in American culture. A 1988 Gallup survey revealed that 80 percent of Americans agreed that "an individual should arrive at his or her own religious beliefs independent of any churches or synagogues" (Gallup 1988). Robert Bellah and associates have noted this increasing spread of an individualistic attitude toward questions of religion and values. They quote a recent political candidate: "I feel religious in a way. I have no denomination or anything like that." The sense of a God of time and history who calls people into community seems to be missing (Bellah 1985, pp. 219–249). Such extreme privatism erodes the sense of connection and support between one's family and the faith community. When some family members hold such an attitude and others do not, the difference is apt to be extremely divisive within the family itself.

The dynamics of each religiously divergent family are unique. Still, there are a number of recurring themes. We have recently been interviewing a number of persons from these families. We will summarize what they told us with this composite story of Sharon and Jim.

Sharon and Jim met when they were young adults. Together they enjoyed sports, outdoor activities, and many common friends. Neither was involved in a church at the time, though Sharon had been active in her childhood and youth. They were married and continued their many weekend activities for the next two years.

Then their first child was born. Sharon recalls, "The marvelous experience of giving birth, then holding the baby in my arms, somehow changed me. Then the memories of being in church with my mother as a small child all stirred within me. As soon as I was on my feet again, I told Jim that I needed to find a church. He didn't like it very well, but he didn't object much either. Sad to say, he didn't come with me."

Thus began a pattern that has continued to the present day. There are now three children, in grade school and high school. Mother and children participate together in worship and separately in selected activities. Father may come to church when his children perform in a choir, play, or musical. Those are the only times.

What is it like to be part of such a family? Sharon responds, "Almost every week, I feel caught in a tug of war. I cannot do as many things with Jim as he would like and still keep any continuity at church. And I can't give of myself to church as I would like. Jim gets upset if I spend many evenings at church activities. I have to pick and choose rather carefully."

What does and can the church do to be supportive to the church participants in such a family? Sharon again: "There are so many things that my church does to make each of us feel included. Worship is a good experience—lots of families are separated during worship. One is in choir and one in the congregation, or the husband is ushering and the wife is seated in the sanctuary. That feels fine. I deeply appreciate each teacher that has taken an encouraging interest in one of my children. That is so important, because my son sometimes wants to withdraw, like his dad. Folks in this church recognized my leadership potential and helped me develop it. I have the friendship support of a lot of people. Some of them come from split families like mine. Some are just folks that I feel close to."

Responding to the question, "Are there things the church does that are insensitive to your family situation?" Sharon replies, "The worst time of the year is the stewardship campaign. I dread those letters coming to our house. Even more I dread callers coming to ask for a pledge. I wish I could give more, and feel guilty that I can't. But I don't think this would be a helpful issue to discuss with Jim."

What can the church do to be open and helpful to Jim, the nonparticipating family member? Sharon's surmise: "The church does beautifully when he comes—quiet, gracious, low-key welcomes without making a big deal over his being there. It would be good to have more contacts from church men who share his hunting, fishing, and golfing interests.

"There was one time when Jim was really impressed with the church. He was out of work, and then, of all things, I had to have surgery. The pastor arrived with a gift of money, unasked. Women from the church brought meals on several days. They'd bring the food, give hugs all around—even to Jim, who hardly knew them—and leave.

That really impressed him. He's been softer toward the church ever since. Still, there's a long way to go. Be patient with all of us. We're doing the best we can. If it ever changes, it will take a long time."

These conversations suggest that the caring Christian church should offer more. Paul speaks of this matter in 1 Corinthians 7:12–16. He affirms that faith and salvation may come to a person through a believing spouse. Churches need to ask how they can help the believing and participating spouses present the gospel directly and indirectly to their partners. Sharon's church may need to hear her wish that Jim might have more male bonding activities with church members. Perhaps someone, or some group, within a church should offer prayerful support for spouses like Sharon, including prayer for the eventual conversion of unbelieving partners.

Faith or Denominational Differences

Another group of families that have religious differences consists of those who marry persons from another faith group. This group includes marriages between:

Persons from different Protestant denominations
Persons from different major branches of the Christian faith
Persons from different major religions

What constitutes a religious difference in a marriage? The answer is twofold: (1) any difference a couple perceives as significant, and (2) any difference that requires a decision on the part of the couple about religious matters. Virtually every couple will have some decisions about religious involvement.

In one of the first weddings at which one of us—Dick—officiated, the couple felt great tension over religion. One partner was Methodist, and the other was Baptist. To ecumenically educated clergy, the difference did not seem great. However, in their small farming community, one extended family all attended the Baptist church and the other extended family went to the Methodist church. Giving up either church was a real sacrifice! In that same community, another couple married for more than fifteen years had never resolved their religious differences. The result was that their junior high children had never been part of a church and wished they could be. In that family, one partner was Presbyterian and the other was Baptist! Again, not a very big difference, except in the eyes of the conflicted couple.

A family with two different religious loyalties can have a continuum of attitudes about their faith commitments: They may be antagonistic to each other's faith, they may be neutral or indifferent, they may be respectful but uninformed about each other's faith heritage, or they may be fascinated with each other's faith journey. Perhaps they will be actively curious about what makes the other tick spiritually. They may resolve that they will claim the resources of both religious communities for their journey as a couple and as a family.

Similarly, such couples or families may choose from a continuum of behaviors: They may be so conflicted they do nothing about either faith commitment; they may be indifferent to each other's heritage, leaving it to the individual to decide whether to pursue it; one or both may elect to change so that the whole family can belong to one church; they may seek a new church that has some continuity and some difference for each member; they may keep up as much participation as possible in both churches; or they may encourage family members to choose their own churches.

There are several other issues. At the beginning are decisions about a wedding—where, what style, and what clergy, if any, will participate? Once married, there are decisions about religious and moral practices—will there be any religious observances in the home and, if so, from what tradition? Whose view of birth control practice will prevail? Each partner may wonder if the other will participate with him or her in personal and spiritual growth and, if so, in what manner. When children are born, there will be the question of religious events to welcome them. Then there will be the issue of religious instruction for the children, possibly including decisions about parochial or public schools. If the family faces crises or tragedies, to whom do they turn for counsel, support, or solace? If persons wish to serve the Christian community in some way, where will that service be rendered? If one wishes to give to the work of the church, how much does one give and to what church?

It is possible for persons of faith and goodwill to face these issues in families. To do so, however, a couple must lay down a foundation early and keep intentional dialogue flowing throughout the years.

Many couples will not feel religious tensions until a child is born. Then each partner may come in touch with cherished memories and hopes for the religious quality of the child's life. At such point, serious dialogue needs to begin.

However, the church's first opportunity to serve such couples may well be on the occasion of their wedding. The clergy have opportunity to help the couple be realistic about the meaning of their religious differences for their marriage. They can encourage the couple to learn more about each other's faith. If the couple wishes, a minister can invite clergy from the other faith group to participate in the wedding. In that way, the clergy can model good relationships with persons of other churches. The pastor can point out the options available. She or he can also put the couple in touch with other interfaith couples who have achieved an effective marital harmony.

The Massachusetts Commission on Christian Unity has prepared a helpful booklet to this end. Entitled *Living the Faith You Share*, the booklet suggests ten guidelines for couples in Roman Catholic–Protestant marriages. In abbreviated form, these guidelines are: (1) Your marriage is holy, (2) your marriage has a special potential, (3) respect what your partner regards as holy, (4) together learn about each other's church, (5) worship God together and as a family, (6) avoid arguing about past history, (7) educate your children ecumenically, (8) don't let the older generation get you down, (9) involve yourself in service to the world, and (10) seek pastoral counsel if you consider changing churches.

Researcher Dolores Curran discovered that couples who live by such guidelines may discover that the diversity of their faiths is an asset, not a liability to their marriage. She identified one trait contributing to family strength as "The healthy family has a shared religious core." However, she noted, a "shared religious core" can be present in a religiously diverse family. She writes (1983, pp. 249–250):

> I . . . find great religious strength in healthy families that are headed by partners who have different religious faiths. . . . I found couples in healthy families who have emphasized the positives in each faith in order to enrich family faith, not destroy it. . . . For example, in union of Catholic and Protestant, the Catholic partner may supply a strong sacramental sense to the marriage while the Protestant partner contributes a better understanding of scripture. . . . Problems in the faith-and-family area stem more from lack of faith . . . than from too many faiths in the family.

Unfortunately, Curran notes, too many couples, when they discover their religious diversity, drop out of any religious expression at all. How important it is for a congregation to be available, loving, and supportive to such couples! In this way it can help them work out the issues of faith in their diverse marriage.

So far, we have been thinking mainly of Christian groups who have some respect for and dialogue with each other. Marriages between persons from these groups have the potential of support and acceptance from clergy, congregations, and family. While it must be admitted that such support is not always there, at least the potential exists.

There are at least two groups of interfaith marriages, however, that present more difficulties. The first group are marriages between persons who do not share as much heritage, scripture, and theology as the groups previously mentioned. The persons' relationship may be complicated further by prohibitions against marriage outside the group on the part of at least one of the religions. Some religions teach that when a person marries outside his or her faith, that person dies and must be treated as dead. In such situations, there obviously will be much less support. Still, the couple may be able to develop a respect, curiosity, and openness to learn more about each other's faith. In such a way a "shared religious core" may be discovered.

The second group of interfaith marriages that present special problems are those in which a partner is a member of a cult, sect, or other dogmatic group that claims it alone possesses truth. Such groups typically assume that error has no rights. In their view, there is only one way to a "shared religious core." That is for the person "in error" to convert to the truth! A most important question for each person to ask a potential spouse is, "Do you respect my spiritual integrity as I am, right now?" If the answer is no, they have little basis for marriage!

When counseling couples with religious differences who are anticipating marriage, it is important to tell each partner, "You cannot love your fiancé(e) without loving his or her faith and church. For that faith and church helped form the fine person you enjoy so much!" The Christian church has both the responsibility and the opportunity to help religiously diverse couples learn how to cope and grow.

Other Religious Differences

There are a number of other religious differences that may exist among members in the same family. For example:

Is religion a matter of challenge and discipleship? Or is it a matter of comfort and convenience? When the claims of a religious group conflict with family interests, which take priority?

Is religion mainly a private resource for one's personal life? Does it have a public dimension, inspiring and challenging the follower to render direct services to disadvantaged persons and to work for the changing of society?

Are a religion's ethical and theological teachings firm, authoritative, true, and binding from century to century? Or are the cultural aspects of the religion's teachings recognized? Is it assumed that in succeeding generations and new situations some teachings may change? Are religious and ethical issues clearly black and white, or are there shades of gray?

Any family that takes its religious quest seriously will not run out of issues to explore together!

Issues of Sexual Values

The tensions families feel over sexual matters are too often expressed by making sexual values a taboo subject. After working through its approach to religion, ethics, and values in general, a family will have a lively time in applying its discoveries to values relating to sex.

Sexual Activity

There are at least three interrelated sexual issues where contemporary families often encounter values differences. The first issue is the sexual activity of unmarried young persons in the family.

Edward Shorter has described a trend toward the younger generation's selecting its own sexual norms. These norms may be in conflict with the values inherited from family, community, and church. He noted that in the late eighteenth century the first major normative change took place—an increased amount of intercourse within couples engaged to marry. The second shift Shorter identified took place in the 1950s and 1960s. This was the "generalization of intercourse," to include the majority of unmarried young adults. From the 1960s on, a fairly high percentage of regularly dating young adults include sexual intercourse as part of their relating. Furthermore, if that relationship proves unsatisfactory, the courtship "dance," including sexual activity, begins with another partner (Shorter 1975, p. 119).

Apparently this trend toward more young people beginning intercourse at an earlier age has continued and accelerated. Social scientists Melvin Zelnick and John F. Kantner have conducted a number of large-scale scientifically reliable studies of sexual and contraceptive behavior of adolescents in the United States. In their 1980 report, these researchers found that half of the unmarried 15- to 19-year-old young women had experienced intercourse (compared to less than one third in 1971). The average age of the first experience was 16. Seventy percent of unmarried males 17 to 21 had had intercourse.

This 1980 study also revealed that, by the time they were 19, 69 percent of unmarried women had engaged in intercourse, compared with 46 percent in 1971 and with 20 percent of the 20-year-old women in Kinsey's 1953 sample (cited in Scanzoni 1984, pp. 31–32).

At least three factors reinforce the decision of many young persons not to follow their parents' sexual norms (or to accelerate trends that began in their parents' generation). (1) There is a new phenomenon in the life cycle, known as "extended adolescence." In 1850, the average age for a child to enter puberty was 16 or 17. That average has been decreasing one year each generation. In 1850 the median age at marriage was 18 or 19 (Stayton 1985, p. 131). In contrast, today the average male has a first ejaculation and the female a first menstrual period at 12 or 13. But the median age for marriage is now 23.6 years for women and 25.1 years for men (U.S. Bureau of the Census 1989, p. 60). Therefore, the transition period between adolescent sexual readiness and marriage has increased from the earlier two to four years to ten to fifteen years. (2) Contraceptive techniques have been developed that allow the separation of procreational from nonprocreational aspects of sexual activity. (Still, particularly in American society, many young people who elect sexual activity do not adequately use contraceptives.) (Stayton 1985, p. 131). (3) Youths live in a society where the public media depict a freer involvement in nonmarital sexual activity. Sol Gordon, when encountering parents who want to be the sole sexual educators of their children, responds, "How can that be? You'll have to wrap your children in cotton and not allow them to leave their bedrooms, watch TV or read newspapers or current magazines. You certainly can't allow them to have any friends or go to any public school bathroom" (Gordon 1986, p. 22).

Persons coming into adolescence will face sexual pressures earlier and more frequently than did most young people of preceding generations. They will face a plurality of sexual practices and sexual values. The families from which they come will, in turn, need to give much thought to what sexual values they communicate.

Nonmarital Cohabitation

There is another decision that an increasing number of young adults make—a decision that may also be in contrast to family values. That is the decision to cohabit with someone before marriage, or without marriage.

This phenomenon is growing rapidly. According to the information given the U.S. Census Bureau, the number of nonmarital cohabiting couples increased 300 percent from 1970 to 1980. By 1980 there were reported 1,560,000 unmarried-couple households. By 1988, the number increased by another million—to 2.6 million. While this represents a fairly small percentage of all households, the number of couples who pass through this status temporarily is far in excess of these figures (U.S. Bureau of the Census, 1989).

Sociologists are astounded at the rapidity of the increase of this practice. One scholar team notes that rarely does any social change occur with the speed that is seen here. They suggest that few developments related to marriage and family life have been as notable as this swift increase in unmarried cohabitation (Glick and Spanier 1980, p. 20).

What has caused this rapid increase? Sociologists can note many contributing factors: the greater sexual freedom among adolescents and young adults, the trend to postpone parenthood and have smaller families, the tendency for marriages to occur a bit later, mobility of young adults, residence in cities and other places of comparative anonymity, increasing acceptance of this practice by society and families. However, they see none of these, nor all of these together, as providing satisfactory explanation for the rapid growth.

Macklin suggests that there are at least five forms of such a relationship: (1) temporary casual convenience—sharing living quarters because it is advantageous to do so, with no presumption of romance; (2) affectionate, going-together relationship—the couple enjoys time together and plans to be together as long as this is true; (3) "trial marriage"—the couple is seriously considering a marital commitment and is testing the wisdom of doing so; (4) temporary alternative to marriage—the couple has made a commitment to marriage but for some reason has chosen to postpone the wedding to a time that seems more fitting; and (5) permanent or semipermanent alternative to marriage—the couple has chosen to live together without legal and religious sanctions (Macklin 1983, pp. 55–56).

For a time it was thought that cohabitation would make an important contribution to the marriages of couples considering that commitment. Some thought that cohabitation might increase marital happiness by screening out some couples who were not compatible with each other. Studies so far have not supported that hope. Several studies conclude there is no evidence that cohabiting couples achieve any better marriage or select partners more appropriately (ibid., pp. 65–67). In fact, one study reported that premarital cohabitation was associated with lower perceived quality of communication for females and significantly lower marital satisfaction for both males and females (Demaris and Leslie 1984, pp. 77–84).

In spite of these discoveries, it is likely that families will have conflict over this topic for some time to come. When parents learn that a young adult child is premaritally cohabiting, what is the appropriate response? If the child is a student with some financial dependence, should parents automatically cut off the support? Should the parents visit their child in the cohabiting home? When the child and cohabiting partner visit the parental home, are they provided one bedroom or two? How do the parents introduce their child's cohabiting partner? Do parents speak out about what they believe on this subject? How many times? Does the kind of cohabiting relationship matter?

Parents need to be true to themselves and speak frankly of their values, while at the same time communicating their love and basic acceptance to their child. Questions of financial support and the etiquette of visitation need to be approached in the light of the kind of cohabiting relationship that is taking place and the larger context of the parent-child relationship. These questions surely deserve open discussion among the adults involved.

What about the church's response to people who take this step? If this behavior is known, are such persons welcome to attend the church? join it? participate in choir and social groups? give leadership in church school, boards, or youth groups? If a premaritally cohabiting couple comes to the minister to be married, is the minister expected to express some religious/ethical judgment? Is the couple to be called to repentance? Or is the minister free to proceed with planning a covenantal wedding service with them?

In our opinion, cohabiting couples should be welcome to attend, participate, join the church, and take part in its activities. We hesitate to give them responsibilities that make them role models for children and youth. As a pastor, Dick feels free to plan a wedding with a cohabiting couple but will usually explore with them whether some remedial work needs to be done in light of their decision to cohabit.

Nonmarital Pregnancies

Out of the sexual activity reported in the two previous sections there were 1,031,000 pregnancies among teenagers in the year 1985. Of these, 31,000 involved girls younger than 15. Pregnancy outcomes included 477,710 live births and 416,170 induced abortions. The remaining pregnancies ended in miscarriage or stillbirth. Another way to state these realities is that 11 percent of women between 15 and 19 had births, abortions, or miscarriages during 1985 (Henshaw and Van Vort 1989, pp. 85–89).

Those are dreary statistics! To add more: The Alan Guttmacher Institute studied teenage sexual activity and pregnancy and concluded that four of every ten females become pregnant before they turn twenty years old. More than one in every ten teenage women get pregnant each year. Forty percent of pregnant teens obtain abortions (Alan Guttmacher Institute 1986).

The high number of nonmarital pregnancies reveals how uneven is the sexual revolution. Although readily available contraception has been a factor in the sexual revolution, there are still a great many unintended pregnancies. For example, of the more than one million teen pregnancies in 1978, 86 percent of them were not intended (Guttmacher 1981, p. 20). Thus, individuals and families face a tragic phenomenon—girls pregnant long before they are ready to welcome children into situations that bode well for the children's welfare.

For families in which there is a nonmarital pregnancy, there are four options to be considered for the young woman: (1) secure a marriage with the child's father and bear the child; (2) bear the child to be raised by the mother as a single parent; (3) bear the child and give it up for adoption; or (4) obtain an abortion.

For some young unmarried pregnant couples, the wise option may be to marry. This may be particularly true if the couple is committed to each other, has been anticipating marriage at some time, and has family support. There should be consideration as to whether each partner has finished or can finish basic and vocational education, and has present or potential employment. Such marriages have a very difficult course. Marriage disruption is two to three times more likely for those who marry while pregnant in their teens than for those whose weddings are in their twenties (ibid., p. 31).

Some young women will give birth to their children while still unmarried to the child's father. At this point, the mother has another choice: to keep the baby or give it up for adoption. To the outsider, it might seem most wise to give the child up. It would appear that this might be best for the welfare both of the mother and of the child. In fact, however, this is rare and becoming more so. Ninety-six percent of unmarried teenage mothers (90 percent of white mothers and virtually all black mothers) keep their children after birth (ibid., p. 27). This represents a rather sharp increase over the last decade of those who are making this choice.

This decision carries a number of serious consequences. There are higher health risks for both mother and child. Quite certainly the mother may discover her educational opportunities, career choices, and future severely limited. The income of young teen mothers is likely to be half that of persons who first gave birth in their twenties. Families headed by young mothers are seven times as likely as others to be poor. Very possibly the young mother will need to claim the resources of the welfare system (ibid., pp. 28–36). A few of the more dire consequences can be averted if the young mother lives with her family and is given family assistance in rearing the child. Still, the consequences of the decision to bear and keep a child as a teenage mother are somber indeed.

There is one other option—abortion. After all the strident debate, it is difficult to gain a perspective on this decision. On the one hand, there is the sacredness of life. Many contend that life should be maintained from the moment of conception. On the other hand, many others acknowledge need for both parents and children to begin their relationship in situations that are optimal for the welfare of all. Many are ambivalent about this issue. Some have said, "I believe in the right of persons to choose an abortion. But I could never have one myself— no matter how inconvenient or troublesome the pregnancy might be for me." Others, confronted with an unwanted pregnancy in an early-teen child, have concluded, "I never believed in abortion, but in this circumstance, it seems like the best possible choice."

There are no absolutely good or absolutely bad solutions—just the best possible in a tragic circumstance. And the fitting solution will vary from situation to situation. As difficult as these decisions are for individuals, they are even worse when family members disagree. If parents and a pregnant minor child disagree about the proper solution, how is it resolved? Do the girl's parents have final responsibility? Or does the teenager herself? What are the responsibilities and the rights of the father and his family? Families in these circumstances need a lot of loving, caring, and listening as they move through the labyrinth of difficult deciding. These are often decisions that have to be made in a hurry!

Not only does the pastor or church leader need to be supportive to the family in this dilemma, the pastor may be drawn into it. If a pregnant teenager confides to her pastor about her situation and asks the minister not to reveal this to her family, what does the pastor do? As pastor both to the individual and to the family, in most circumstances clergy will do well to urge young persons to confide in their families. (Exceptions would at least include abusive families and cases of incest.) The decisions to be made for one's present and future are too weighty for one to decide in isolation from one's family in most circumstances. Families are generally supportive, once they survive the initial shock. There is little to be gained in keeping the facts secret from the family.

Other Value Issues in the Sexual Area

There may be other issues some families face. For example, a family member may announce to the family that he or she is homosexual. Usually the family had not considered this issue before being told. Suddenly they are confronted with a number of value questions. Is this family member sinful, sick, or living out an ethically viable and healthy option? Does the person have a choice about his or her sexual orientation, or is this just the way it is? What is basic—the person's sexual orientation or the person as someone loved and valued by the family?

The Rev. Bruce W. Morgan, copastor of First Baptist Church, Dayton, Ohio, has been drawn into ministry with persons with AIDS and their families. This began when he was informed by his youngest brother that he was suffering from this illness. He recalls, "We family members discovered what it is like to love someone unconditionally and came to appreciate the role of caring and loving in sustaining life." By phone and direct visit, Morgan's family has drawn together in mutual support.

At the same time, a member of his congregation contracted this illness. He comments, "Our church had the opportunity to put its faith commitments into practice by upholding, loving, and supporting one of our members during the period of his illness with AIDS and through his death. There has been a total absence of judgment and condemnation, and a generous outpouring of love. The gospel is alive and well in the church."

As an extension of his personal commitment to persons with AIDS and witness to the church's compassion for those who are ill, Morgan has been drawn into many areas of service. He participates in the Dayton AIDS foundation, which raises money to provide housing, transportation, legal counsel, food, a hotline to information and referral, spiritual guidance, counseling, and education. It is their goal that nobody who is ill with this disease go unattended in a time of special need. He has also interpreted opportunities for ministry to others and networked with other churches making a similar commitment. He notes that churches provide support groups, counseling, homemaker care, drop-in centers, prayer, and worship services for healing, transportation, and more. He suggests, "This is a time for the church to be in the vanguard. When AIDS strikes within a family, there is trauma, grief, fear, and an overwhelming anxiety about the future. Thankfully, those of us who live by faith, and who understand God's healing to be a spiritual as well as a physical reality, do not despair and do not turn from the one with the special need. Rather, we respond with love and care and stand together in the ministry of healing. In our family, all have grown in the quality of love and devotion we feel toward one another. Even AIDS has united us and bound us to one another in uncompromising commitment."

Other Values Differences

There are numerous other values differences that may occur in families. Some are more subtle than the ones we have already noted, but these also can be a source of family stress and pain.

There are a variety of value issues related to finances. What is responsible financial living—to avoid debt as much as possible, or to live up to one's line of credit? How important is saving? To what extent should persons accumulate a financial cushion against possible crises? How important is it to pay one's bills? to do it on time? How significant is it if one defaults on loans, files bankruptcy, or has one's vages garnisheed?

There may be values differences involved in the topic of aging. Do older people hold the wisdom of the nation and thus merit great respect and reverence? Or are they inconvenient anachronisms who can't keep pace with the fast changes of today and tomorrow? How should they be treated? What attention should be paid to their opinions and advice? (In the eyes of some, older people may be those over 40!) Other cultures and times have answered these questions in different ways. How will we handle this issue in our family?

There is a parallel issue here: What do we mean by family, and what part of the family is worthy of our loyalty? Is it our nuclear family only? our extended family? our family kinship network? What role do grandparents have in our family?

What are the work values in our family? Is work something in which to take pride, something that gives dignity to the person doing it? Or is it a necessary evil, the way one gets a paycheck? Does all work need to be done well, as nearly perfectly as possible? Or is some work just not worth that kind of attention? What sort of loyalty, reliability, dependability does one owe an employer?

And how do we achieve some balance between work, leisure, and contemplation? Do various family members value work most highly, leisure most highly, or contemplation most highly?

How does a family handle values with regard to self and society? What is the individual's most basic imperative—to find oneself, know oneself, make something of oneself? Or is it to give oneself? How are people helped to handle our culture's twin tugs of altruism and "meism"? Which is most basic, and how can each balance the other?

If the needs of the group and those of the individual conflict, which take priority? And if the needs of the group are given consideration, which group—family, school, church, peer group?

And what is the family's attitude toward society? Does one accept society, adjust to society as it is? Or does one try to change it? Does love of one's country mean little or no criticism of its leaders and policies? Or can these be widely discussed, criticized, and protested?

What is the family's attitude toward pleasure? Should fulfillment be as immediate as possible? Or should some pleasures be delayed from childhood to youth, or from youth to adult years? What is responsible parenthood in regard to immediate and delayed gratification?

How does the family handle value issues themselves? Is this subject not discussable, as values are firm and unbending? Perhaps the values come from one's family, nation, Bible, or culture; they are clear and need only be obeyed. Or are values circumstantial, situational, varying with new experiences and demands? Are there some central values while other topics are open to further exploration? And what is the norm for dealing with differences about the values themselves?

Value conflicts in families may be the fastest-growing area of family concern. There is so much questioning and rejecting of authority, such pluralism of choices, so many new options for the young. And yet, it is an area in which churches seem to offer little help. Perhaps families and churches can discover ways to relate ancient wisdom to new questions and challenges. If so, the church has the potential of helping families deal with their religious and value conflicts.

Family and Church Respond to Values Conflicts

Adults in families can work at developing their convictions about values—their source, their meaning. In this connection C. S. Lewis contended there is one judgment of values that is embedded in all the major civilizations of the world. He suggested that universally there is a moral stance that includes the following judgments (quoted in Strommen and Strommen 1985, p. 106):

The "law" of mercy
The "law" of magnanimity (generosity in forgiving; willingness to die for another)
The "law" of doing good
The "law" of caring for one's family (duties to parents and others; duties to children)
The "law" of justice (sexual justice; honesty; justice in court)
The "law" of good faith

Lewis suggested that over the centuries a consensus has evolved as to what is moral, good, or of value. This morality is revealed and raised to a new level in the Old and New Testaments. He contended that the "human mind has no more power of inventing a new value than of imagining a new primary color, or indeed, of creating a new sun and a new sky for it to move on" (Strommen and Strommen 1985, p. 106).

Merton and Irene Strommen suggest there are two levels of moral behavior: (1) trying to know and obey the basic values of a moral universe, and (2) attempting to rise above such laws and the expectations of others to a new level of responsible living (ibid., p. 110). There are basic values and values of aspiration. While in-depth Christian discipleship leads one to values of aspiration, it is unreasonable for parents to expect that of their children. Parents may want to encourage it and inspire it, but that level of commitment and living will need to be freely chosen by the child.

If what we said about the moral structure of the universe holds true, this does not eliminate the values confusion of which we have been speaking. In decision-making, one value may conflict with another, and usually does! In a complex value system, one needs to develop a priority of values.

Parents' most pressing question might be "how": How do parents communicate values to their children? If church leaders understand that, they can help equip parents for this all-important process. Actually, some things are known about how values are communicated in families. Here are eleven aspects of value communication:

1. Through love. Unconditional love to a child, love that does not need to be earned, forgiving love in the presence of moral lapses, is a key ingredient in communicating values.

2. By example or model. Parents and others who regularly embody what they believe—and who can acknowledge when they fall short of their aspirations—offer a powerful impetus, perhaps on the preconscious or unconscious level.

3. With consistency. Married parents need to develop consistency between them. Each moral communicator will need to seek consistency between what one expects of self and of others.

4. In words. Parents will need to state what they believe and live by and what they expect of their children. They will do this best if they do it informally, frequently, in short sentences and small doses.

5. Through accountability. Children are taught to live with the consequences of the decisions they make. Moral mistakes (such as stealing) will need to be confessed and amends made.

6. With recognition of intent. Sensitive parents can sometimes better discern intent than behavior. Such intent needs to be recognized and affirmed even as better means to achieve it are mutually explored.

7. By encouragement to live morally. Parents can be prime encouragers for the child or youth who wants to choose a moral course but fears peer disapproval. One mother gives her daughter permission to blame her: "My mother won't let me." Young persons need our awareness of their desire to do what appears right and still to be liked. And they need settings in which to work out those dilemmas when they must choose one or the other alternative.

8. Through lively discussion of how values are reached. Sidney Simon and associates have created the field of "values clarification" in which persons learn together the process by which they choose values. These educators have created a number of exercises and discussions that enable a family to enjoy learning about one another's value choices. Such experiences might take this topic from the "heavy" atmosphere that often pervades discussions of morality and open up conversation by exploring less threatening areas first.

9. With awareness of how moral development takes place. Lawrence Kohlberg and associates have explored how moral thinking develops from early childhood. They note a progression from an awareness of punishment . . . to a stage that is more preoccupied with what satisfies one's own and others' needs . . . to a time when the person wants to please others and be approved by them . . . to a stage where morality is to maintain the social order and do one's duty. Some

may develop to even more mature perspectives than those. The point is that the parent with awareness of this information may relate to a child on an appropriate level and not expect more than the child is able to consider at a given age.

10. Through open examination and discussion of cultural values, particularly those communicated through the media. The Strommens' studies revealed that those children with much unexamined exposure to mass media exhibited more than the average amount of hedonism, use of drugs and alcohol, sexually arousing activity, and rejection of traditional moral beliefs (Strommen and Strommen 1985, p. 115). Since children and youth cannot be isolated from this world, conversation and second opinions about such matters need to be shared within the home.

11. With trust. No parent can live his or her child's life or control that child's decisions as the youngster moves into youth and young adult years. Letting go lovingly, with faith in one's child to make wise, responsible decisions—such might be quite an impetus to value-filled living!

If we have adequately described the family opportunities for communicating values, the church is able to be of help. The church can provide the forum where uncomfortable issues can be examined and defused. Courses on comparative religions and ecumenical marriages; discussions on sexuality in the light of Bible, theology, church history, and contemporary issues; skill groups for the parent as the sexual educator of one's children; introductions and practice sessions on values clarification and moral development; media awareness workshops—these and other opportunities can be developed within the adult and family-life education program of a church. We call on churches to undertake: (1) clarifying the congregation's position, (2) adult education aiming at insight and clarity about religion and values, (3) parent education offering insight and skills about religion, morality, and value communication, and (4) support to parents and families.

Even with all these efforts, there will be times when children will act out strong differences from their parents' values. At such times parents will need to discover how to forgive themselves, support each other, and live with the pain. A gifted pastoral counselor, herself the parent of young adult children, once said, "Of all the pains of parenting, the greatest is the pain when our children reject our values."

This is another opportunity for church family and other friends to be quietly supportive and accepting. We can be transparent about how many of us belong to that fellowship of those who have suffered through such value conflicts. Together we can say to the suffering parents, "Hang in there. We are with you. And you know, one thing is sure. The next chapter in your family history will have to be better!"

Resources and References

Alan Guttmacher Institute. 1981. *Teenage Pregnancy: The Problem That Hasn't Gone Away.* New York: Planned Parenthood Federation of America.

_____. 1986. "United States and Cross-National Trends in Teenage Sexuality and Fertility Behavior." Unpublished data.

Bellah, Robert, et al. 1985. *Habits of the Heart.* Berkeley, Calif.: University of California Press.

Bishops' Committee for Pastoral Research and Practices, National Council of Catholic Bishops. 1989. *Faithful to Each Other: A Catholic Handbook of Pastoral Help for Marriage Preparation.* Washington, D.C.: United States Catholic Conference.

Chamblin, Joseph M. 1979. *Together for Life.* 2nd ed. Notre Dame, Ind.: Ave Maria Press.

Curran, Dolores. 1983. *Traits of a Healthy Family.* New York: Ballantine Books.

Demaris, Alfred, and Gerald R. Leslie. 1984. "Cohabitation with the Future Spouse: Its Influence Upon Marital Satisfaction and Communication." *Journal of Marriage and the Family*, February, pp. 77–84.

Dryfoos, Joy G. 1985. "A Time for New Thinking About Teenage Pregnancy." *American Journal of Public Health*, vol. 75, no. 1 (January), pp. 13–14.

Fraenkel, Jack R. 1977. *How to Teach About Values.* Englewood Cliffs, N.J.: Prentice-Hall.

Gallup, George. 1988. *The Unchurched American . . . Ten Years Later.* Princeton, N.J.: Princeton Religious Resource Center.

Gaulke, Earl H. 1975. *You Can Have a Family Where Everybody Wins.* St. Louis: Concordia Publishing House.

Gilligan, Carol. 1982. *In a Different Voice: Psychological Theory and Women's Development.* Cambridge, Mass.: Harvard University Press.

Glick, Paul C., and Graham B. Spanier. 1980. "Married and Unmarried Cohabitation in the United States." *Journal of Marriage and the Family*, vol. 42, no. 1 (February), pp. 19–30.

Gordon, Sol. 1986. "What Kids Need to Know." *Psychology Today*, October, pp. 22–26.

Gordon, Thomas. 1970. *P.E.T. Parent Effectiveness Training: The Tested New Way to Raise Responsible Children.* New York: Peter H. Wyden.

Henshaw, Stanley K., and Jennifer Van Vort. 1989. "Teenage Abortion, Birth and Pregnancy Statistics: An Update." In *Family Planning Perspectives*, vol. 21, no. 2 (March/April).

Kohlberg, Lawrence. 1966. "Moral Education in the Schools: A Developmental View." *School Review*, Spring, pp. 1–30.

Larson, Roland, and Doris Larson. 1976. *Values and Faith: Value Clarifying Exercises for Family and Church Groups.* New York: Harper & Row.

Macklin, Eleanor D. 1983. "Nonmarital Heterosexual Cohabitation: An Overview." In Eleanor D. Macklin and Roger H. Rubin, eds., *Contemporary Families and Alternative Lifestyles.* Beverly Hills, Calif.: Sage Publications.

Massachusetts Commission on Christian Unity. Undated. *Living the Faith You Share.* Needham Heights, Mass.: Whittemore Associates.

Paolucci, Beatrice, Olive Hall, and N. Axinn. 1977. *Family Decision Making: An Ecosystem Approach.* New York: John Wiley & Sons.

Scanzoni, Letha Dawson. 1984. *Sexuality.* Philadelphia: Westminster Press.

Schiappa, Barbara D. 1982. *Mixing: Catholic–Protestant Marriages in the 1980s.* New York: Paulist Press.

Shorter, Edward. 1975. *The Making of the Modern Family.* New York: Basic Books.

Simon, Sidney B., and Sally Wendkos Olds. 1976. *Helping Your Child Learn Right from Wrong.* New York: Simon & Schuster.

Simon, Sidney B., Leland W. Howe, and Howard Kirschenbaum. 1972. *Values Clarification: A Handbook for Practical Strategies for Teachers and Students.* New York: Hart Publishing Co.

Stayton, William R. 1985. "Religion and Adolescent Sexuality." *Seminars in Adolescent Medicine*, vol. 1, no. 2 (June), pp. 131–137.

Stinnett, Nick, and John DeFrain. 1986. *Secrets of Strong Families.* New York: Berkley Books.

Strommen, Merton P., and A. Irene Strommen. 1985. *Five Cries of Parents.* San Francisco: Harper & Row.

U.S. Bureau of the Census. 1989. *Marital Status and Living Arrangements: March 1988.* Current Population Reports, Series P-20, no. 433. Washington, D.C.: U.S. Government Printing Office.

6

Couples Without Children

In our exploration of changing families, we now direct our attention to those without children. These families fall into two major groups: those who are childless involuntarily and those who choose to be child-free.

Involuntary Childlessness

To begin, let's consider folks who are childless during part or all of their marriages because of natural circumstances.

Rick and Jo Ann, an Older "Childless" Couple

Rick and Jo Ann pull their station wagon into the driveway, having delivered their youngest child to college.

This couple had married in their early twenties. They had three children born in the first seven years of their marriage. Now they are in their late forties, and the last child has left. Child care in some form has occupied their attention for twenty-four of the twenty-six years they have been married. Now, for all practical purposes, they are childless. They will still maintain interest in their young adult children, and they hope for grandchildren someday.

However, the responsibility of parenthood that claimed much of this couple's attention, energy, and time, is almost over. Rick and Jo Ann have a good chance of spending as many years together after children as they have spent with children.

Somehow, the community to which they return seems different from the one they left that morning. When they left, the heavily loaded station wagon had scraped on the driveway. On the way back it bounced and rattled. It now feels like an obscenely big gas eater for two people. The house—the one they'd bought with a large rec room in their carefully chosen school district—that house now feels as if it was built for someone else.

They pick up the newspaper in the driveway and look at their mail. Somehow the news about school bond issues and school board elections seems less interesting. Their church newsletter has a plea for church school teachers and for increased giving so the youth minister can be retained. Though Rick and Jo Ann wish their church leaders well, those issues have lost some of their tug on them. The rest of the church newsletter has little that interests them. Has the church always been that child- and youth-centered without their noticing it?

Rick and Jo Ann putter around the house, catching up on some neglected chores. Each is tired from the day's activities but also filled with sadness and uncertainty. Both ponder life after children. They remember what friends have told them—that when children leave, a marriage either gets better or gets worse. Which will it be for them? There are going to be some holes in their lives. What is going to fill them?

With the aging of the population, Rick and Jo Ann represent a growing group of adults whose concerns the church is likely not addressing. What will it take to change the church's response?

Jo Ann and Rick are childless in the natural course of events. Children do grow up and move on. Middle-aged couples usually grieve their loss in this transition and then adjust to a new relationship with offspring who have become adults with their own agendas. But other couples find themselves childless throughout their marriages because of natural barriers to conception. Theirs is a greater and more painful challenge.

Kaye and Craig, a Couple Facing Fertility Problems

Kaye and Craig were married shortly after their graduation from college. Kaye recalls that she married Craig because of the double attraction of her personal love for him combined with her conviction that he would be a terrific father. Both assumed that they would start bearing and raising children as soon as they were settled.

Their early married years were just what they wanted them to be. This was a time to establish careers, to found a home, to enjoy each other and get to know each other better.

After two years, they were ready for the children, so Kaye went off the pill. But she did not become pregnant—not in the first year, nor in the second.

They started working with gynecologists and fertility clinics. Kaye was advised to start taking her basal body temperature and check back in a few months. Then there were tests for both Kaye and Craig, followed by medications. Kaye recalls, "We also learned of and tried to control many other factors which can affect conception: having a good breakfast, drinking little alcohol, not smoking, controlling weight, taking warm rather than hot showers, and Craig wearing shorts rather than briefs. We tried everything, becoming more and more impatient.

"Our sexual relations became extremely frustrating. Having sex for its own sake was impossible, because timing became essential. Conflict arose between sexual desires and rational desires to conceive a child. I felt a growing sense of personal inadequacy and a whole gamut of other negative feelings relating to infertility" (Halverson 1980, p. 47).

All this was bad enough. Worse was that many of their couple friends (who seemingly broke all those rules) were conceiving effortlessly!

They next went to a well-known fertility clinic. In time, following the advice of the specialist, Kaye underwent a laparoscopy and laparotomy. She was in surgery for five hours. The doctors found extensive endometriosis, a build-up of tissue in the uterine lining that makes it extremely difficult to become pregnant. Following this ordeal, she was instructed to go on the pill again for another nine months to keep the endometriosis under control.

In the midst of all these efforts to conceive, Kaye and Craig filed application with an adoption agency.

While they had been active in church during much of this time, even helping with the youth group, they now found themselves withdrawing. It was hard to field questions about plans for children. Kaye found herself angry with a God who would withhold a child from persons who could be such good parents. She experienced long periods of depression.

She recalls an event during a vacation weekend. "One night after an elegant dinner, I cried hysterically because I felt so worthless. I wasn't a mother; I was a failure. I wasn't a good teacher any more; I was a failure. I wasn't a good wife, as I couldn't give Craig a child and I couldn't even let him enjoy his vacation; I was a failure. I wasn't a good daughter, as I couldn't give my parents a grandchild; I was a failure. A total failure as a woman and a human. What purpose did I have, anyway?" (Halverson 1980, p. 74).

Time continued to pass. Her close friend and support person in fertility matters asked her to share that couple's joy when they received their adopted child. Her younger sister became pregnant. Kaye and Craig accepted the option of attempting artificial insemination with the husband's sperm. This was very difficult for her. It seemed so "cold, unloving, sterile, and extremely difficult emotionally." She questioned it religiously. But she underwent three series (each included five straight mornings of artificial insemination). Each time there was the hopeful wait, and then, each time, monthly menstruation. This was followed by great disappointment and depression. "Finally we agreed we could no longer go on with this. . . . At my next appointment I told the doctor we wanted to discontinue artificial insemination, and then I totally broke down, crying uncontrollably." Her doctor's stern, confronting words at this time led her to conclude: "I knew I must learn to cope with our reality—our infertility. I must put my trust in God and accept my life" (ibid., pp. 82–83).

Gradually she and Craig found the means of coping. After some painful times, Kaye achieved a breakthrough in communication with her parents and family about their pain in regard to the infertility. It felt so rewarding to be able to talk with caring family members about all that was going on in her life. Kaye also underwent a career change—from teaching, where she felt rather burned out, to interior design. As a couple, they provided child care for two weeks for two toddler children of dear friends who needed to explore a new employment opportunity. Craig and Kaye also took training in foster parenting. Eventually, they discovered that while it is an option for some persons, it was not for them.

And, remembering how alone they had felt in so much of this, Kaye resolved to write a book. She would tell about their struggles and the growing perspective and acceptance of their infertility. She hoped through the book to help others struggling with similar problems. At the same time she discovered that the writing was good therapy for her. She and Craig were charter members and became involved in an organization called RESOLVE, which lends support to persons struggling with infertility. The story we have told is a brief summary of the book she wrote. It is entitled *The Wedded Unmother*.

After they had been married for nearly ten years, and after being on a waiting list at an adoption agency for nearly seven years, and after having tried valiantly to overcome infertility and, not achieving that, gaining perspective on their feelings—a phone call came. A social worker inquired if they were ready to begin final processing to await the adoption of a child. They decided they were, and after some more long, agonizing months of waiting finally received their adoptive daughter, Heidi Marie Halverson.

The Halversons are well aware that adoption is just one of many ways for a couple to resolve infertility. Each couple will need to find its own way.

Issues for Persons Who Are Involuntarily Childless

We now move from the Halversons' personal story to consider general themes in involuntary childlessness. We shall start by exploring the term "infertility." A common definition of infertility is "the inability to conceive a pregnancy after a year or more of regular sexual relations without contraception, or the inability to carry pregnancies to a live birth" (Menning 1977, p. 4). Estimates are that 15 percent of the population of childbearing age is infertile at any one time. This means that one in every six or seven couples who are of childbearing age—more than ten million people in the United States alone—are struggling with this problem. It is important not to confuse the terms infertility and sterility. Sterility may be defined as permanent, incurable infertility. Many who are infertile have conditions that can be treated, and in some cases corrected. It appears that infertility is a problem that has grown considerably, from perhaps 5 percent of the population to 15. There may be many reasons for this increase. Some forms of birth control, the trend toward delaying marriage and childbearing, and the increase in venereal disease are some of the reasons cited (Halverson 1980, pp. 96–97). Currently the possibility that environmental toxins contribute to infertility is being explored.

Barbara Eck Menning suggests that since many ill-informed myths exist around infertility, it is important to debunk these myths with accurate information. (1) *"Infertility is not a 'female condition.'"* An analysis of diagnoses reveals that in about 40 percent of the cases women have the problem. In 40 percent of the cases men have the problem. The couple shares the problem in 20 percent of the cases. (2) *"Infertility is not usually due to psychological factors."* In 90 percent of the cases a physical problem is found. The remaining 10 percent have problems not at present diagnosable or treatable with current technology. (3) *"Infertility is not incurable."* For couples who enter competent diagnosis and treatment, 50 percent respond to treatment and conceive. (This is in contrast to only 5 percent of couples who "spontaneously conceive" without treatment after having been infertile for a year.) (4) *"Infertility is not a sexual disorder."* For most couples, infertility has nothing to do with capability in sexual relations. (5) *"It is not immoral or irresponsible to want to bear children and to work at it."* Even though the world has a population problem, children are wanted and needed for the world's future. Couples should bear children responsibly, out of free choice, if they so decide. Infertility represents the denial of the right to choose (Menning 1977, p. 5).

When a couple discovers that it will be difficult or impossible for them to have a child, very likely they will experience a life crisis. On one level, they may respond by seeking the best medical help available to them. As described in Kaye and Craig's vignette, treatment may start rather simply—timed intercourse based on the female's cycle as indicated by basal body temperature, and selective use or nonuse of the pill. If this fails, more complicated and invasive procedures may follow.

While infertility usually does not arise from the couple relationship or sexual problems, contending with infertility can put a strain on the couple. The following is a copy of the actual orders one infertility specialist gave his patients (ibid., p. 127).

1. You will shake down the rectal thermometer, place it on the bed stand, and set the clock radio for the same time each morning.
2. You should get to bed at the same hour each night.
3. Avoid use of alcohol or smoking if possible.
4. In the morning, when the alarm goes off, the husband should gently awaken the wife and insert the rectal thermometer for five minutes.
5. When the temperature is taken, they may go back to sleep if they wish.
6. The couple will have sexual relations on the nights of days 11, 13, 15, 17 each cycle.
7. Sexual relations at other times may be whatever the husband wishes.

While that specialist's list might be both overly rigid and sexist, it does indicate factors with which such a couple must contend. Not surprisingly, such instructions may be troubling to a couple. One man comments, "I feel I must *produce* [sexually] at a specified, clinical, predetermined moment, when the act of sharing love with a wife is something that should be natural, unplanned, spontaneous."

Another couple recalls, "We felt like we always had someone between the sheets with us. First and foremost there was the thermometer. Then the doctor. We felt at various times as if both sets of our parents were in the bed with us. And finally, during adoption, the social worker seemed to join us in the bed. During this whole time we have never had that bed to ourselves" (ibid., p. 126).

At the same time that they are undergoing treatment, the couple is dealing with feelings that arise out of the infertility. These feelings will become more intense if it is discovered that the infertility is not treatable and is permanent. The range of feelings may include:

• surprise that this problem exists for them
• denial
• isolation, for even in this day of sexual candor many persons either do not feel able to discuss infertility or else make inappropriate, uninformed, hurting remarks, which increase the sense of loneliness
• anger, which may have many objects: medical professionals, spouse, self, God, insensitive people, and more

• guilt and unworthiness, seeking a cause in something they did or did not do, or wanting to atone for past mistakes (they may attempt to bargain with God)

• depression, either normal depression, which is perfectly natural, considering the loss of cherished hopes and dreams, or pathological depression, masking even more powerful and frightening feelings that the person does not feel ready to face (ibid., pp. 104–109).

This list of emotions sounds like a classic description of persons in grief. And indeed, when a couple discovers that its infertility is incurable, there is a grief process that must be endured.

However, as Menning points out, this grief has complications that may cause the normal healing process to fail. For one thing, there may be no recognized loss. Persons involved may not be aware that it is appropriate to grieve the loss of a potential person. People who could be supportive may not be aware of the loss. Furthermore, the loss may be "socially unspeakable." Overladen with guilty feelings and possible sexual overtones to the loss, some persons cannot bring themselves to talk about it. Further still, there may be a degree of uncertainty. A slim thread of hope may remain, however unrealistic. Also, there may be social negation of the loss. Even if the loss is known, most persons expect that the ones involved will keep quiet about it. And finally, there may be the absence of any support system of meaningfully related people (ibid., pp. 112–113).

For a variety of reasons, then, the permanently infertile couple may find it difficult to resolve the feelings that surround their circumstance. Still, they need to have worked through those feelings so they are ready to consider their alternatives. The good news is that there are viable alternatives. A couple can find their way to a rich, meaningful life, once they have resolved their feelings and accepted the conclusion.

One of their alternatives might be adoption, perhaps of an international child or a child with special needs. Or they may want to be foster parents, either in relationship to a social agency that needs to place children temporarily or as a haven for exchange students. If the infertility resides with one partner, they may consider artificial insemination; in the scenario just provided, the insemination was with the husband's sperm. There is also the possibility of finding a surrogate mother for the husband's sperm. This provides genetic continuity for one person in the couple, but this is an extremely complex issue, with personal, moral, legal, and practical concerns. Some legal experts are urging that there be no more surrogate mothers until the rights of all are clarified legally.

The couple may choose child-free living, with all the variations of creativity that this option includes. There are two important biblical/

theological teachings that a childless couple may want to claim. One is that we are creative children of a creator God. God's creation is more than procreation, and so is ours! The creation of ideas, art, systems, relationships, and more is available to each person who is in the image of the creator God.

The other biblical teaching is that God's call comes not only in the positive experiences of life. It also comes in the failures, the losses, the closed doors. The call out of such experiences might be to sensitivity and caring for persons undergoing similar struggles. Or it might simply be a clarifying moment to reveal what one's call is not. Then a person is ready to go on and discover what that person's call is.

Jesus of Nazareth procreated no children, but who was more creative? Meaningful vistas of creativity and call beckon to the childless couple who have moved beyond their pain.

The Voluntarily Child-free

Our exploration now undergoes an abrupt transition. While persons in the preceding group greatly desired children and reluctantly accepted their childless fate, the next group elects to be child-free. Two stories will move us into this topic.

Yvonne and Elaine, the Early Child-free

Yvonne and Elaine spot each other in the company cafeteria and find a place where they can eat together. With unaccustomed difficulty they slide into their booth. Both are pregnant, both for the first time. Yvonne is thirty-eight years old, and Elaine is forty-two. Their conversation quickly changes from company events to how they are weathering their respective pregnancies. Funny, they had never noticed before, but company maternity leaves are really not very generous at all.

Yvonne tells Elaine about going in for ultrasound and amniocentesis tests to be sure that her baby does not have Down's syndrome. A former special ed teacher, Yvonne is sure that she couldn't be the parent for a multiple-problem child. She is concerned about the possible greater risk for pregnancies in older mothers. All tests are fine. As an added benefit, she now knows that she will have a boy. Elaine and her husband decided not to have the tests. This is probably their only chance. And though mindful of the age risk, they want this child, whatever.

They reflect on their past and their present. Both came into young adult years in a time when there were improved birth control methods and freedom of choice. Yvonne was glad for that. Her first marriage was so unsettled there was never a secure time to start a family. The marriage became more troubled. Then there was the divorce and singleness. Eventually she remarried, and in time the new marriage was beginning to feel stable enough to welcome a child. The years had gone by in all of this, and now she and her husband felt a sense of urgency. The present time is their only opportunity.

For Elaine, it was different. She and her husband had both enjoyed their careers and had put much of themselves into these efforts. Their combined incomes had given them freedom to relax and travel whenever busy careers allowed. They had not so much decided against a child as delayed the decision. In fact, they delayed it for years.

On her fortieth birthday, Elaine felt a vague emptiness that grew more urgent with the passing months. She and her husband chose a first pregnancy when some of their friends were packing their children off to college.

The two friends inquire of each other's plans. Yvonne plans to go back to work after the three-month maternity leave—at least for a while. Elaine says she plans to apply for half-time work—at least for a while. Both agree that though they made these decisions maturely, they have not fully absorbed all the changes that are coming. The transition from having been child-free couples to child-rearing will be complex indeed.

What messages does the church give couples like these who choose to put career ahead of child-rearing, at least for a few years? How does the typical church program speak to their concerns as young adults who choose to live without children for at least part of their married lives?

Yvonne and Elaine and their spouses made the decision to have children after many years of child-free living. Some couples make the decision to be child-free throughout their marriages.

Ted and Nicki, Mark and Liz, Two Child-free Couples

When Evelyn, associate minister at First Church, was invited out for a leisurely breakfast with senior pastor Ron, she suspected she knew why. Probably Ron had another issue that was troubling him—something where he needed either a listening ear or a second opinion.

Ron was in the last decade before his retirement. He held in high regard his able associate who was nearly twenty-five years his junior. Somehow their combined insights and wisdom had been useful in helping First Church steer a course that embraced tradition and contemporaneity.

As usual, Evelyn was right. After their order was taken, Ron sighed deeply and exclaimed, "I don't know if I did the right thing." Evelyn waited and Ron went on. "When Ted and Nicki came to me to be married, they said there was something they needed to tell me. Since they are both so serious about their music careers, they have decided they will not have children, ever. They told me that their creativity will be expressed on the music composition sheet and the keyboard, not in the obstetrics ward. Their 'children,' so to speak, will be their work. With their priorities, they didn't feel they would be good parents. Children would feel like an intrusion on their life passion.

"I was surprised. Certainly people should be wise and careful in the timing and number of their children. But this was the first couple to tell me up front of their plan not to have children.

"Later, I was preparing their service and writing their prayer. I became aware of how much wording I had to change. Then I became uncomfortable. It seems that the Christian church has assumed that marriage is a commitment to childbearing. I'm not sure that I should alter that or cater to persons' whims."

Evelyn sat quietly for a few moments. "I have faced the same issues. A few months ago while working with Mark and Liz, I encountered an extra variation. Mark told me loud and clear there would be no children. I turned to Liz and asked how she felt. She shrugged helplessly and responded, 'I don't want children soon, but my feelings could change.' Then I asked Mark, 'Is this a forever decision, or could it be discussed at a future time?' He responded, 'We can discuss it, but my feelings will not change.' None of us had the tools to get beyond that impasse. They both agreed that in spite of this, they wanted to proceed with their wedding plans, and so we did. I had a sinking feeling. I feared that this reproductive freedom was going to bring pain to them sometime in the future."

Ron thought out loud: "Maybe the church ought to stay out of this whole thing. I've never agreed with the Roman Catholic teaching that lack of desire for children is a valid basis for annulment. However, at least they have a position. They state clearly that children go with marriage."

Evelyn shook her head in disagreement. "I doubt that is the way to go. As a matter of fact, I know couples who are models of responsibility and mutuality who don't have children.

"Besides, my biblical theology of marriage does not assume the necessity of children. I think the marriage covenant is about two people making commitments to each other before God and community. That does not necessarily imply the promise to beget children."

"My goodness, you're right," Ron answered. "We have assumed that since the culture expected fertile couples to have children, so did God. And that might not be the case at all. Not for everyone. Ted and Nicki's plans seemed right for them. I was uncomfortable because I hadn't worked out my theology on this issue."

Ron felt better. "Some of us have some relearning to do. And, I suspect there is a good bit of reeducating we need to do in church and community as well."

Issues for Persons Who Are Child-free

Perhaps many of us are in the position of Ron. We need to gain some handles—historical, theological, personal—for dealing with issues regarding people who choose to be child-free.

Certainly throughout history there have been couples who sought to avoid childbirth. For the most part, though, this was not a highly visible or discussable matter.

In the rather recent history in our country, during the depression decade of the 1930s, spinsterhood, delayed marriage, and small families (when possible) were common. Lifetime childlessness approached 20 percent. Quite possibly economic deprivation and pessimism about the future contributed to those low birth rates (Burgwyn 1981, p. 3).

It was in the 1960s, however, that this issue burst upon American consciousness and demanded attention and response. A survey in 1960 carried out by Robert Blood and Donald Wolfe in Detroit revealed that couples childless by choice were practically nonexistent (Blood and Wolfe 1960).

Then the feminist movement came to prominence. It proclaimed several influential themes—the dignity of the woman in herself, her right to freedom of choice, her right of access to the occupational marketplace, her control over her own body. At the same time, birth control methods became more diverse, reliable, and convenient. To the condom and diaphragm were added the IUD and the pill. If one wanted to postpone or refuse pregnancy while still having sexual relationships, one could.

In this environment, a few persons started speaking out for nonparenthood. In 1963, Gail Greene wrote an article in the *Saturday Evening Post* entitled "Speaking Out: A Vote Against Motherhood," in which she described life without children as being "wondrously satisfying." (Her article drew three thousand letters, most of them angry.) In 1969 Stephanie Mills, valedictorian of her class at Mills College, California, announced in her commencement speech her intention to remain childless. She said, "I am terribly saddened by the fact that the most humane thing for me to do is to have no children at all" (Faux 1984, p. 1). A year later, Betty Rollin wrote an even more outspoken article in *Look* magazine, "Motherhood: Need or Myth?" She suggested, "If God were to speak to us in a voice we could hear, even He would probably say, 'Be fruitful. Don't multiply'" (Burgwyn 1981, p. 8).

These influences and opinions stimulated both experiments with child-free marriage and further thought and discussion. In the 1970s a number of notable thinkers questioned the "maternal instinct." Some parents began to feel as defensive about their decisions as some non-parents had felt about theirs. Polls raised the question of parental satisfaction. The most widely publicized was an admittedly unscientific survey by Ann Landers, who asked her readers, "If you had it to do over again, would you have had children?" She received 10,000 answers, and more than 70 percent said "No!" It should be noted that a few years later *Better Homes and Gardens* did its own survey and found that 91 percent of the parents who responded said that they *would* have children again (ibid., pp. 11–12).

While enough years have elapsed so there is perhaps more balance in the discussion of such issues these days, there is a clear trend. Many couples are having their children later, having fewer, and in significant numbers having none at all.

In May 1980, the U.S. Census released a report that revealed the rapidity of this change. From the years 1960 to 1980, the percentage of childlessness among women age 20 to 24 who had ever married increased from 24 percent to 41 percent. Among women age 25 to 29 who had ever been married, the percentage of childlessness increased from 13 percent in 1960 to 25 percent in 1980 and to 27 percent in 1986 (U.S. Census Bureau 1988, p. 8). Some demographic experts are predicting that as many as 25 percent of the women now of child-bearing age will remain permanently childless (Burgwyn 1981, p. 22). As a matter of fact, in 1987, 24 percent of women in their early thirties had not had a child, up from 20 percent in 1980.

A study by the Roper Organization in 1980 made the surprising discovery that while 94 percent of American women favor marriage, 82 percent do not feel that children are essential for a marriage to be happy (ibid., p. 17).

Having a child has become a decision, not an assumption. What causes some couples to decide "no"? The motives are undoubtedly varied. Authors on this theme underline the seriousness of this decision. In exploring *The Child-Free Alternative*, Kate Harper offers her assumptions (1980, pp. 4–5):

> I believe that those who have children should have them by informed choice. I believe that children are too precious to be created out of unquestioning acceptance of roles, expectations, or doctrines. I believe that simple failure to consider the alternative is no reason to have children.
>
> I think that we have come to a significant crossroads in human life, one that may determine whether we will continue to be able to live on the earth. I think that those who choose to work on solving our enormous social,

ecological, and moral problems are deserving of support, respect, and acceptance. If not having children is part of their contribution, I think we must respect that choice, even if we do not agree with it.

I believe that all of us are part of one family—the human family—and that all of us must choose our own way, fully aware that all choices involve some kind of loss. Finally, I believe that if someone simply doesn't want to have children, that's reason enough for them not to have any.

Diana Burgwyn adds, "Of all the decisions people make in a lifetime, none is more crucial than the one to become a parent or remain childless. . . . A child regretted is not returnable, and one desired too late will not be born" (Burgwyn 1981, p. 65).

There seem to be two pathways by which persons arrive at a decision to be or remain child-free. Jean Veevers discovered that about one third of childless wives had entered marriage with a firm commitment to childlessness. Many of these had developed strong feelings about this in early adolescence before ever seriously considering marriage. The other two thirds of her study population postponed parenthood to some future time—a future that did not come.

She discerned four stages in this process. In the first stage, the couple postpones children for a definite period of time. In the second phase, the couple remains consciously committed to parenthood, but the "when" of parenthood becomes increasingly vague. In the third phase, each partner in the couple admits privately, and perhaps to the other, that they might not have children at all. In the fourth stage, the couple does decide not to have children. This is probably precipitated by the awareness that they should have their children by a given time or not at all. This decision may be marked by voluntary sterilization on the part of one partner, or it may not. They may want to keep their options open a little longer. But the decision appears to have been made (cited in Whelan 1975, pp. 129–131).

For those who gradually move through such decisions, there seem to be two tugs. There is a pull toward something other than parenthood. Some persons discover they want to do something other than parenting with their time, energy, talent, money, or education. Some are aware of the strain on our ecosystem and social systems. Others find themselves drawn toward building a relationship with their mate Some want to make a wholehearted commitment to career.

There is also a pull away from parenthood. Some people are not particularly attracted to children. Others may fear that because of their own inadequate home environments as children (abusive or addictive parents, for example), they will not be good parents. Others find themselves with no partner at all, or a partner without any interest in childbearing. They sense that, while they might have elected parenting at another time with another partner, it does not seem fitting now (Harper 1980, pp. 166–167).

When Burgwyn interviewed a number of child-free couples about their decisions, she heard the following reasons among their responses. A frequent theme was "freedom." This included freedom to pursue career, to maintain a life of spontaneity and mobility, to continue one's education, to take risks. Closely related was the topic of career goals and the need to make a wholehearted commitment to career. Money was yet another consideration. There was an awareness of the cost of children and of the possible need to give up one income for a time to care for children. Intimacy and the special nature of the couple's one-to-one relationship was frequently mentioned. She discovered that some of the couples interviewed were very nurturing people, who chose to lavish their nurture and their intimacy on a spouse. Popular folklore has promoted the idea that it is the family with children that is the happiest. Actually research on this topic is not without contradictions. Indications are, however, that voluntarily childless marriages are at least as happy as those with children. These are the themes that Burgwyn heard while perceiving that there may well have been other underlying reasons for some of their decisions (Burgwyn 1981, pp. 28–66).

A significant number of couples have elected to be child-free because of their other commitments. These persons are, on the average, as healthy individually and at least as healthy as couples as are the childbearing. The decision not to have children has not had adverse effect on them as individuals or as couples. They will have some special joys and possibly some particular regrets. They live in a society that has become somewhat more accepting but does not yet know how to be entirely supportive and understanding.

The Church's Response

One more descriptive detail needs to be mentioned about couples without children—both types. Not many couples without children are found in churches, even those who have had devout upbringing. Quite possibly this is because they do not sense a hospitable environment for them at church.

The term "pronatalist" is used in discussions of the non-childbearing question. It simply means "in favor of birth," and may be taken to mean that bearing children is seen as essential and central to marriage. Roman Catholicism, Judaism, Mormonism, and Protestant fundamentalism have all been perceived as being strongly pronatalist.

While liberal or main-line Protestantism has claimed to provide an environment in which all responsible ethical issues can be explored, that has not been apparent to childless, or child-free, persons.

One woman told us, "I find the church's response to this to be almost totally nonexistent. In their eyes, being childless is almost as bad a stigma as being single. There is no warmth or mercy shown to childless couples. This is tragic and needs to change." We hope that such experience is not widespread, but we are afraid that it is.

The first thing the Christian church will need to do is work on its theology of childlessness and child-free-ness. At first glance, this may seem a difficult thing to do. It would appear that biblical teachings lie on the side of childbearing. As O. J. Baab has noted, in Bible times the view seemed to be that only by bearing children could a woman achieve her true purpose in life. "Barrenness" brought sorrow, regret, disdain. One's children are like "olive shoots" around the family table, a sign of God's favor (Ps. 128:3). Grandchildren are "the crown of the aged" (Prov. 17:6). Sarah, Hannah, and Elizabeth come to mind as biblical figures who sorrowed in their childlessness and rejoiced in childbearing (Baab, p. 558). Children carried on the family name, identity, and hope for the future. While that thinking may have fit an ancient agricultural society, it needs to be questioned in our day.

Concerning biblical theology, there is room for another word to be spoken. While recognizing the delight and joy that children can bring, there are at least four possible items in a theology of childlessness: (1) Each child created in the image of God deserves to be born into a home that has the time, interest, and resources to provide for it. Life agenda or lack of resources may mean that not every couple is ready to take on this task. (2) In a world of mushrooming population, scarce resources, and tremendous expenses in childrearing, children should be begotten thoughtfully, not spontaneously. For some this may mean raising a smaller family; for some it may mean having no children. (3) A person can have worth or dignity without being a mother or father. When a woman cried out to Jesus, "Blessed is the womb that bore you, and the breasts that you sucked!" Jesus responded by saying, "Blessed rather are those who hear the word of God and keep it!" (Luke 11:27–28). In other words, you don't have to be someone's mother to find meaning in life. You can find it by believing, acting, living in relationship to God. Persons can be creative without being procreative. (4) A marital relationship can have worth and dignity without children. The Bible's most basic statement about the purpose of marriage is "Therefore a man leaves his father and his mother and cleaves to his wife, and they become one flesh" (Gen. 2:24). This passage speaks to the deep oneness, harmony, and community that two people can experience in a marriage blessed by God. It does not speak of children. In these and undoubtedly in other themes, there is room to explore a theology for both the voluntarily and the involuntarily childless.

Having done this, church leaders need to look at their own assumptions, festivals, and programs for a pronatalist bias. One involuntarily childless woman felt such bias at Mother's Day and other family life services in her church. She felt pain in the unthinking praise of motherhood and felt ignored because of her circumstance. In the vignettes, Ron found such bias in the marriage he performed. Rick and Jo Ann discovered it in their church newsletter.

Not only will church leaders need to examine existing church rituals and services, they may need to create new ones. For example, the Rev. Nancy Gieseler Devor tells of a request to her from dear friends: "Help us with some grief work. Would you help us to do a memorial service for Isaac—the child we will never have?"

These friends had gone through the long process of attempting to overcome infertility. Finally, they had realized that they would not succeed, and it was time to let go and mourn their loss.

And so Devor provided an occasion to allow her friends to do that. They spoke of their hope and of the name they would have given their child. They described their struggle. She asked them to reflect on how acceptance of this reality would change their lives. What dreams would they let go, what new dreams were they now free to form? Then they held hands and prayed, "We return to you the potential of this infant life, which for us simply will not be—and which even now is being laid to rest. But more important, we commit to you the potential in our own lives." Then they hugged and cried, and eventually experienced God's peace and strength.

Devor points out that the church needs to stand ready to offer such aid to the one in six couples who may experience infertility. She is aware that she and her husband may need such help one day. "We will need the chance to mourn and pray, to be healed and to renew our trust and dedication. We will need the church then, as surely as we will need it should we experience the joy of new life, of giving birth to our own baby, our own Isaac" (Devor 1988, p. 391).

A ministry that has extensive outreach to couples having difficulty in conceiving and bearing a child is "Stepping Stones," an outreach of Central Christian Church in Wichita, Kansas. This unique ministry began in 1980 when three women in the same Bible-study group discovered that they all were praying for children. They reached out to each other for mutual support and began looking for spiritual resources to help them deal with infertility. Sadly, there were very few resources at that time. One of their pastors suggested to them that they develop such resources, and they set out to do just that.

The volunteer founders of this ministry—Lynn, Leslie, and Janet—

found numerous ways to fulfill their purpose: "to offer hope, encouragement and support to infertile couples."

Their goals are to educate the public and the church about the special needs of infertile couples, to help such couples to know that they are not alone and that they may reach out to each other in prayer and mutual support, to help infertile couples strengthen their marriages and understand themselves as family, to guide infertile couples in God's word and God's principles so that they can have positive attitudes and trust in God, to offer information about medical advances in the field of infertility, and to be a clearinghouse for information on seminars, meetings, books, and articles on infertility and/or marriage enrichment.

Their main instrument for accomplishing these goals is a bimonthly newsletter, *Stepping Stones*, which contains a variety of materials—articles giving information or emotional support, testimonies, poetry, book reviews, and notices of events of interest. Circulation is now forty-five hundred, reaching persons in twenty countries. Prepared by a volunteer staff and funded by contributions, this publication is sent free of charge to any who request it.

In addition, this ministry offers counseling by phone and letter, helps people to reach out to one another as pen pals or phone pals, and offers its expertise at various conferences and gatherings.

While considering such outreach, a church may also want to ask itself some hard questions. Is our program tilted toward children, youths, and the families that include children or youths? Do we offer personal growth opportunities for individual adults? for couples, regardless of whether they have children?

Sensitive leaders may want to rethink their evangelism with persons in their twenties and thirties. The "old practical wisdom" used to be: "Many young adults will withdraw from church life for a while after high school. Don't worry. They'll be back when they are married and start having babies." If the forecast is accurate that 25 percent may elect child-free-ness, what might the church have to offer them? Is it possibly more healthy when one is an adult to choose a faith and church for oneself, rather than for the sake of one's children?

Another thing that the church can do is to help open up the dialogue on the subject of childlessness. Even in this day of freer discussion on sexual matters, there is still relative discomfort about the subject of childlessness. The church can help break this barrier of silence. Perhaps at a family-life forum a childless couple could be included. Possibly this couple could help church people know of these issues, of the insensitive things that too often people say to the childless, and of ways to be sensitive and caring to childless folks. It might be that church leaders should know whether local chapters of RESOLVE, Inc.

(for the involuntarily childless) and support groups for the child-free exist. If not, perhaps church leaders will want to create them to meet needs of persons in the community. If such groups do exist, church leaders can refer people to them and invite speakers from them.

Committees of Christian education might send out persons to interview folks without children in the church. Questions such as these might awaken new possibilities: How is the church doing with you? In what ways are we meeting your needs? In what ways are we not? What sensitivities, what insensitivities do you experience here? Do you have friends without children who do not participate in a church? How could our church be more attractive to them?

Youth groups need the opportunity to explore the issues of optional parenthood. These might include at least two aspects of their lives. Youth might be helped to think about life goals and possible ways to achieve their goals. For both males and females, the question of where children fit, or do not fit, into these goals needs to be raised. Also, the responsibilities of parenthood can be explored. Perhaps a youth group could sponsor a structured learning experience similar to those assigned in public school family-life classes: Youths (individually or in couples) are given something that represents a child. Sometimes the "child" is an egg, sometimes a five-pound bag of flour. The couples must keep this "child" with them or make provision for its care every moment for an entire week! This provides rich opportunity to discuss decisions about parental responsibility.

Young married groups might welcome the opportunity to discuss how one makes decisions about children in the light of today's reproductive freedom.

In all of this, perhaps the church can help overcome the feeling that many childless people mention as they speak of feeling alone in these matters. They are not alone, but bridges need to be built, among childless couples and between them and other caring folks. Surely, church folk can be such bridge people.

Resources and References

Baab, O. J. 1962. "Child." *Interpreter's Dictionary of the Bible*, vol 1. Nashville: Abingdon Press.

Blood, Robert O., and Donald M. Wolfe. 1960. *Husbands and Wives: The Dynamics of Married Living*. Glencoe, Ill.: Free Press.

Burgwyn, Diana. 1981. *Marriage Without Children*. New York: Harper & Row.

Devor, Nancy Gieseler. 1988. "A Service for Isaac." *Christian Century*, vol. 105, no. 13 (April 20), p. 391.

Faux, Marian. 1984. *Childless by Choice*. Garden City, N.Y.: Doubleday & Co., Anchor Books.

Halverson, Kaye, with Karen M. Hess. 1980. *The Wedded Unmother*. Minneapolis: Augsburg Publishing House.

Harper, Kate. 1980. *The Child-Free Alternative*. Brattleboro, Vt.: Stephen Greene Press.

Houseknecht, Sharon K. 1982. "Voluntary Childlessness in the 1980s: A Significant Increase?" *Marriage and Family Review*, vol. 5, no. 2, pp. 51–70.

Menning, Barbara Eck. 1977. *Infertility: A Guide for the Childless Couple*. Englewood Cliffs, N.J.: Prentice-Hall.

RESOLVE. 5 Water Street, Boston, MA 02174, Telephone (617) 643-2424.

Stepping Stones. Bimonthly newsletter, 1982 to present. Available from Stepping Stones Ministry, 2900 North Rock Road, Wichita, KS 67226.

U.S. Bureau of the Census. 1988. *Fertility of American Women: June 1987*. Current Population Reports, Series P-20, no. 427. Washington, D.C.: U.S. Government Printing Office.

Veevers, Jean E. 1980. *Childless by Choice*. Toronto: Butterworth.

————. 1983. "Voluntary Childlessness: A Critical Assessment of the Research." In Eleanor D. Macklin and Roger H. Rubin, eds., *Contemporary Families and Alternate Lifestyles*. Beverly Hills, Calif.: Sage Publications.

Whelan, Elizabeth M. 1975. *A Baby? . . . Maybe*. New York: Bobbs-Merrill Co.

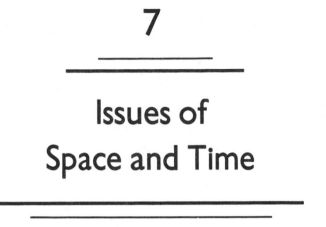

7

Issues of Space and Time

When is a family a family? And when is it not? For a long time social scientists have answered that at least one basic characteristic of a family is a common residence. G. P. Murdock defined the nuclear family as a "social group characterized by common residence, economic cooperation, and reproduction." D. Schneider added, "The family, to be a family, must live together" (cited in Gerstel and Gross 1984, p. 7). The U.S. Census Bureau defines family as persons related by blood, marriage, or adoption, sharing a kitchen. Many would probably conclude that, whatever may be lacking, if a family has a place to be together and spends time together in that one space, that grouping is a family.

Can exceptions to this understanding of the family be made? In our culture we have understood that there were some necessary exceptions. Some persons have to travel for their work, salespersons, business executives, entertainers, over-the-road truck drivers, and seasonal employees, for example. Others serve in military service. Occasionally one member of a family that wants to migrate from one place to another goes ahead to become established. In due time, perhaps months or even years later, the family follows.

In these exceptions, there has been a widespread assumption that the necessarily absent member is the male/husband/father. The necessarily present member is the female/wife/mother.

The number of families that live with issues of presence and absence, of time and space, seems to be growing. And the kinds of reasons for this time-space problem are growing. Also, no longer is there such a clear-cut distinction between who may travel and who must stay "home."

There might be a variety of metaphors for this type of family:

> The accordion family, often squeezed for time, occasionally stretched out over a good bit of space
>
> The cafeteria family, where members drop by from time to time to select what they need to keep going
>
> The bed (once in a while) and board (occasionally) family
>
> The family that "invests" in phone companies and airlines but receives emotional, not financial, dividends.

We will examine a number of family situations with issues of space and time.

Commuter Marriages and Families

What is a commuter marriage? It is a dual-career marriage in which both partners feel a strong commitment to their respective careers. In order for each to pursue optimal career development, they establish separate homes in separate places (Gerstel and Gross 1984, p. 7).

How does such a decision come about? When commuter couples are asked, they tend to respond that they just fell into it, or it was the only logical thing to do, or that the pattern just evolved.

Naomi Gerstel and Harriet Gross, who have extensively studied commuter marriages, see a more complex process at work, however. They consider the key factor to be the woman's entry not only into the work force but into a meaningful career commitment and profession. A second element is the husband's history of transfers for career advancement. In these previous moves, the wife followed the husband and attempted to adjust her career to his. This pattern risks several unsatisfactory results. For one, the wife's career is interrupted, and she has to start over again in a new place, often at a lower level. Or she finds herself underemployed. She may take a large cut in pay and in self-esteem for the work she does. Possibly she finds no work in her area of expertise. As a result of all this she experiences considerable unhappiness and depression, which in turn affect the couple's and family's life.

This scenario may lead the couple to reexamine their "unsymmetrical" view that the husband's career always has precedence. Such soul-searching may prompt them to seek locations that have opportunities for both. Or it may cause them to agree on giving priority to their place of dwelling, even at the cost of career advancement.

There is much about the workplace that makes the pursuit of two careers by marital partners difficult. Some companies have policies against employing both spouses. Few companies offer sympathetic help for dual-career couples. Consequently for some couples there are no solutions that allow them to work at full capacity in the same community.

An increasing number of couples elect a commuter marriage because of their commitment to each of their careers in equal measure, and at the same time commitment to their marriage. *Because* the married partners place this high value on both career and marriage, they may choose to live apart for some of the time (Gerstel and Gross 1984, p. 47). While it may not be viewed by the couple or by others as a good solution, given the job market and other social conditions it may be for some the only solution (ibid., p. 51).

Because the Census Bureau does not record this style of marriage, it is difficult to know how widespread it is. There are estimates of at least 700,000 commuter couples (Winfield 1985, p. 4).

Who are the couples who make this choice? They are, of course, a diverse group. The couples vary in age, length of marriage, whether there are children, and if so, in their ages. There is also variety in the distance they live apart and how often they can see each other. And there is a wide range of financial circumstance, and thus in what they are able to spend to keep in touch with each other and to be together.

For the most part, however, commuter couples seem to be persons with high educational levels, high-ranking occupations (professionals, academics, executives), and therefore at least somewhat higher than usual income levels (Gerstel and Gross 1983, p. 182).

What is life like for folks once the commuter marriage decision has been made? There are losses, gains, and changes that "just are." These changes occur within the individuals, within the couple/family, and between the couple and other persons and institutions.

On the loss side of the ledger, couples speak of the loss of "trivia talk." They miss the chance to have someone with whom to share the joys, sorrows, and humor of their day. They sense a decrease of emotional support. They did not realize how much they valued just being together in "shared inactivity"—simply being around each other for an occasional break as each pursues his or her interests within their home setting. Persons miss the shared home setting itself. Some (apparently more men than women) become aware that marriage has some order-producing and meaning-producing elements that they miss when alone. They find themselves not as productive as they had thought they would be. More time is spent procrastinating and daydreaming.

While couples attempt to compensate for these losses with journals, letters, tapes, and phone calls, none provides an entirely satisfactory solution. They discover that there is no substitute for personal presence and adequate time for reflection, feedback, or conflict resolution (if necessary). Nor are there those spontaneous opportunities to go to a movie, have a laugh, make love. As a result, some find themselves avoiding touchy or conflict-laden topics.

Commuter spouses experience decreased sexual satisfaction and activity with their partner. Of course the distance contributes. Even when together, there is always the press of time. Many things need to be crowded into the weekend visit. Both may be fatigued from the week or the commute. Some experience the "stranger effect"; couples relate that it takes a while to get used to each other again (experienced more by women than men). Interestingly, surveys of commuter couples do not indicate increased extramarital sexual activity.

Long-distance couples also discover decreased contact with mutual friends and other social groups. And they do not, in the rush of their present schedules, find themselves striking up many new friendships. They find that our society is often segregated into married and single, and "married singles" do not fit into either grouping.

These couples often face disapproval and doubt about the strength of the marriages. Repeatedly they encounter the suspicion that the choice of separate residences is a step on the way to divorce. Even relatives and friends often express disapproval. Such disapproval seems to be on two grounds. For one thing, it is seen as not "macho" for a man to "allow" his wife to live independently. The other criticism is that this is no way to raise children.

Some changes in commuter marriages may be considered as loss by some people and gains by others. For example, the separation of tasks by sex role—domestic chores, yard work, child-rearing—is often broken down. Both spouses must undertake whatever work needs to be done. Less attention and effort seem to be given to each of these tasks by both members.

All of this is much more complex if there are children still at home. Then one partner labors with issues similar to the overloaded single parent. The other parent experiences an acute sense of missing important events with the child(ren) and of guilt over doing so.

There are, however, positive gains as well. The most obvious is the unfettered career development of each partner. Whether this means simply gaining entrance into a field with limited openings, or being able to accept the promotions, raises, and increased responsibility that may come from performing well, this factor is a significant plus.

Persons discover some gains in their couple relationship as well. These are the "flip side" of the couple losses. There is an avoidance of the depression and despair that a partner may feel from living in a community where that partner does not want to be and which often has no career opportunities for the partner's gifts. If the day-to-day contact between spouses is missed, there is increased attention to each other and to the relationship in the time that the couple can be together. Each partner has had time to pursue individual interests while apart. Couple/family tasks and interest may occupy the time they are together. There are fewer "trivial arguments." With awareness that everyday contact has led couples to boredom and despair, the infrequently together couple is motivated to give each other more attention and energy. To be sure, time together may carry a subtle pressure to make it good time and avoid upsetting issues. Still, couples tend to become less habitual and more intentional about their couple relationship.

There are some factors that can make commuter marriage more manageable. A reasonably strong marriage that has had some time to develop strength certainly helps. If the distance is small enough (or the finances great enough) so that spouses can see each other frequently, weekly if possible, then a commuter marriage is a less negative experience. Some conditions of work may help. For example, if either or both partners are academics, they may have extended time together during vacations from the school year, which allows some catch-up time with each other. If they can compartmentalize work and family time so that when together they can really be together, that contributes to a manageable lifestyle. Some find comfort in seeing the situation as "temporary," even though they are not sure when it will end.

These two-residence marriages have many issues to face that make it a difficult arrangement. And yet it can be manageable, and for some even rewarding (Gerstel and Gross 1984, pp. 134–155).

Sociologist Eli Ginzberg has suggested that the dual-income family may become the most important social change of the twentieth century (Winfield 1985, pp. 85–86). This change will undoubtedly lead to a variety of other changes in family life, of which the commuter marriage is but one. Gerstel and Gross, while seeing commuting as a necessary arrangement for some, have one other observation worth noting: "But we, like commuters themselves, would rather see a world where career demands cost less, and responded more, to the family life of women and men" (Gerstel and Gross 1984, p. 202).

Military Families

Couples and families that have at least one member in military service also live with issues of space and time as well as some other dynamics.

Approximately eleven million persons are attached to the military in some way (active duty, reserves, and dependents of such persons) (Hunter 1986, p. 62).

The military family (and attention to this family) is a relatively new factor in military history. In earlier periods of time, the military was considered the domain of the single man. In 1847, Congress specifically prohibited enlisting men with wives and/or children. While there have always been "camp followers" attached to many military groups, and while these might include wives and children, such hangers-on were only tolerated. No provision was made for their welfare.

During World War I, conflicting policies on military families were in effect. While marriage was strongly discouraged, the first system of family allotments was instituted. During World War II, Congress took steps to recognize the needs of the family by increasing allotments and adding some obstetrical care. In the fifties, programs were developed to strengthen family life, with the awareness that this would contribute to retention of military personnel. In the 1970s, major federally funded research revealed many unique needs of military families and led to establishing family service centers on major bases (Hunter 1986, p. 61).

Women in military service had yet other problems with which to deal. For years, military regulations required the mandatory involuntary discharge of any servicewoman who became pregnant or otherwise assumed parental status (including stepparenting). This regulation ended in June 1974 (York 1978, pp. 75–87). Now, a relatively brief time later, there are indeed servicewomen with children. Some of them are married to servicemen and share the considerable problems of handling assignments and care for the children while each parent fulfills military obligations.

Edna Jo Hunter points out the implications of the increasing number of military families that are single-parent families or have working wives, including those in which both spouses are on active duty. In 1970, 30 percent of wives of military personnel were employed outside the home; by 1980, it was 65 percent. This change has meant a decline in the number of potential volunteers to aid in various kinds of community service. Also, employment of spouses has increased the problems involved in a transfer of assignment, similar to those faced by civilians (Hunter 1986, p. 63).

There are two frequent facts of life for military persons and their families: transfer (where the family possibly may follow them), and deployment (where the family may not accompany them). Let's look at these in turn.

On the average a military person (and his or her family) is transferred once every two to three years. (There is a move to lengthen assignments to at least four years on stateside assignments in the army.) These assignments may be to bases in other parts of the United States or to other parts of the world.

This frequent change of domicile has its problems and its positive aspects, both for the children and for the adults. Recently the Norfolk (Va.) *Virginian-Pilot* and *Ledger-Star* newspapers published a questionnaire which they invited wives of active-duty navy persons to answer. There were 1,800 responses. These wives mentioned the frequent transfer as the most difficult aspect of their marriages.

For the children the difficult aspects are leaving friends (mentioned by 33 percent); going to a new school (mentioned by 28 percent); making new friends (mentioned by 24 percent); and adjusting to new surroundings (mentioned by 13 percent).

Frequent transfers mean repeated attempts for children to become established and make friends in a new neighborhood, climbing on a new school bus full of strangers, and starting many aspects of their lives over again. These changes also mean rootlessness. Said one mother, "They have no roots. They're from *nowhere*." A child may pause when asked where she or he is from. The moves may be so frequent the child does not know. Some parents report that while they negotiated these moves fairly easily when the children were small, the moves were more difficult when the children became teenagers. It seemed that old friends were missed more acutely and new friendships were harder to make in this stage of life. Parental attitudes toward the move are important to children of all ages.

For spouses there is also the separation from friends, as well as a number of other tough issues. Losing one's job and having to look for a new one over and over again may be demanding. Many experience discrimination in job-hunting since employers presume they will be short-time employees because they are military spouses. Finding new housing and financing the move are heavy responsibilities. Though there are allotments for moving expenses, most agree that moving costs them substantially more than what is paid. Then, with the constant uprooting of frequent moves, some are hesitant to make close friendships or commitments to community, church, or other organizations. (Others have learned to join in quickly.)

The gains for adults and children are similar. "I enjoy meeting new people," said one wife. Others comment, "It keeps your heart and mind open. . . . It has been positive as much as it has been difficult. We can't go anywhere but that we don't know someone there. [Our] two daughters have been educated as much by our moves which included stays in Europe and the Orient, as by anything they have learned in school. . . . We have been places most people never see." Those who are able to see the frequent moves in a positive light use words like "adaptability" and "flexibility" rather than "instability" and "rootlessness" to describe their family experience (D'Orso 1988).

While the transfer involves the entire family moving together, another fact of military life, deployment, involves a military person's leaving his or her family behind for a period of time to fulfill an assignment.

The frequency and length of deployment vary greatly with the branch of service and the type of assignment. And, of course, they vary between peacetime, war, and times of crisis or emergency. Since the determining factor is military need, the schedule for deployment may be postponed or moved up, shortened or extended. In some deployments there is fear for the safety of the persons involved. Thus, the family's uncertainty about the time schedules of deployment is compounded by anxiety about a loved one's well-being.

Some aircraft carrier crews routinely have six months of deployment every two years. For some submarine crews, it may be alternately three months on shore and three months of deployment. In the army some assignments may be for six or twelve months. If one goes without family to an area where family could accompany one, however, the deployment may be twenty-four months.

For all who experience deployment—the military person, the spouse, and the children—there is a series of adjustments each time it happens—anticipating, experiencing, recovering from it. Kathleen Logan has studied this process and has discovered a seven-stage "Emotional Cycle of Deployment" (ECOD). Her original study considered navy wives, but she has discovered parallel processes in husband and children as well.

Before this cycle begins, though persons know the deployment is coming, they tend to ignore it, to fantasize that it will be canceled, to push it out of mind. At some point there is a recognition that the day of departure is coming. This is the point where the cycle (the ECOD) begins.

Stage one: Anticipation of loss begins four to six weeks before the actual time of departure. Emotions begin to build up. A spouse may find herself crying at times, angry occasionally. In addition, she may feel unproductive, restless, depressed, irritable. There is an attempt to get many tasks done that require the husband's assistance. The woman may feel resentful: "He's really going to leave me alone with all this." And the man may feel guilty: "There's no way I can get everything done that I should before I leave."

Stage two: Detachment and withdrawal take place in the final days before leaving. There may be a sense of despair or hopelessness. This is accompanied by the feeling that the marriage is in someone else's control, not the couple's. A wife may express the sentiment, "I know I should be enjoying these last few days together, but all I want to do is cry." There may be some ambivalence about sexual relations. This is tied to the pain they feel knowing that they will not be together again for a significant time. If one partner desires sexual closeness and the other feels the need to draw back, this may be a further source of tension. The couple may share fewer feelings and thoughts with each other. During these first two stages, abuse cases increase.

Stage three: Emotional disorganization occurs right after deployment, and perhaps for six weeks following. Though they may think they are ready, the actual deployment comes as a shock. There may be a sense of relief, soon replaced by nonproductive restlessness, sleep disturbance, confusion, disorganization, irritability. The emotional unspoken question is, What am I going to do with this "hole" in my life? Ordinarily this too is a temporary phase. Unfortunately, some persons become stuck at this stage, unable or unwilling to move on. They will have problems for the duration of the absence, and perhaps beyond.

Stage four: Recovery and stabilization begin following stage three, and are of variable length, partly dependent on length of deployment. The mood is "Hey, I'm doing OK!" The spouse establishes family patterns, settles into routines, reorganizes roles and responsibilities. Ongoing decisions and tasks are faced, emergencies are handled. Support is found through friends, church, work, wives' groups. One observer calls these the "single wives" (reminiscent of the "married singles" described in the discussion of commuter couples). Spouses in stage four may in some ways find it a time of growth, a surprising benefit of this lifestyle. For many, it is an opportunity to initiate new activities, accept increased responsibilities, and stretch themselves and their abilities. For others, there may be a dark side to stage four. Some feel much stress, may be sick more frequently. There may be continued mild depression and anxiousness. But for the most part, they experience increased independence, freedom, self-confidence.

Stage five: Anticipation of homecoming starts to take shape roughly six weeks before the end of deployment. The recognition dawns that a reunion will soon take place! This is accompanied by mixed feelings—joy, excitement, eager anticipation on the one hand, and apprehension, questioning, uncertainty on the other. It is a time when some partners reevaluate the marriage. It may be a time for the waiting spouse to draw back from some involvements to make room for the marriage relationship. The wife may be wondering, Will he understand and accept the changes that have occurred in us? Will he approve of the decisions I have made? Will he adjust to the fact that I can't go back to being dependent? The husband will have his own questions: How have we changed? How will I be accepted? Will the kids know me? Does my family still need me? At some point in this activity of questioning, the persons involved find their readiness for the next stage.

Stage six: Renegotiation of the marriage contract is experienced during approximately six weeks following deployment. Together physically, couple and family need to work on getting together emotionally. After time together, sharing experiences and feelings, doing things together, eventually they begin to feel like a family. There is the need to refocus on family. Changes in schedule come about ("I have to cook a real dinner every night! How about you cooking once in a while?"). The wife may need to live with feelings about shared responsibility and the loss of independence and solo leadership. The couple will need to find a pattern for working out differences. If there is tendency to spouse abuse or child abuse, it may appear in the tenseness of this adjustment. Some feel they have cleared the air after their first argument following return and reunion. Sexual relations, though eagerly anticipated, may seem tentative and frightening at first. The couple will need time before they can expect true intimacy. Logan comments, "This stage can be difficult as well as joyful. But it does offer an opportunity offered to few civilian couples: the chance to evaluate what changes have occurred within themselves, to determine what direction they want their growth to take, and to meld all this into a renewed and refreshed relationship" (Logan 1987, p. 46).

Stage seven: Reintegration and stabilization take place over time, a month or two after the reunion. Gradually the couple comes to feel like "we" and "our" again. Husband and wife feel relaxed and comfortable with each other and with the new routines established for the family. A sense of being couple and family reemerge. There is opportunity to enjoy the closeness and warmth of a good marriage (ibid., pp. 43–47).

However, even after successfully completing such a reintegration, many military families having ongoing problems to face. One of these is the role of the military father. With recurring absences at each stage of his children's lives, what is his role? During these absences, the relationship of mother and children changes. Sometimes they grow closer and depend more on each other. Or perhaps the children will have problems of behavior, emotion, or discipline connected to family issues. Their relationship to their father will change also. Small children who do not understand why their father left may feel abandoned. Very young children may even forget their father while he is gone. All children will grow and move on from one type of interaction and discipline to another.

Fathers often have two understandable temptations when they get home. One is to be the "softy"—the gift giver, the playmate, the one who indulges and spoils his children. The other is to step in rather suddenly and correct behavior and discipline patterns that don't feel right to him. While both are understandable, probably a more modest, middle-of-the-road approach is wiser. As each one learns the experiences of other family members, mother and father can come together gradually to evolve their parenting style while the father is home.

In summary, the military is an institution that for most of its history excluded and ignored families. With its recent accommodation to and emphasis on caring for families, there is still much about it that poses real stress and threat to families. Still, it is in this setting that families attempt to develop the flexibility needed to develop a strong family lifestyle while dealing with issues of space and time.

The Involuntarily Institutionalized

The issues confronting families with institutionalized members are in some ways similar to the issues faced by those living with military deployment and reunion. However, the cycle experienced by families with institutionalized members is even more unpredictable. Perhaps the absent family member was hospitalized with a mental illness. Or it could be that the member was convicted of a felony and sent to prison with a sentence of time that must be spent there.

At the beginning, both the one institutionalized and the other family members must adjust to the change. Then they need to find ways to be in touch. The institution may have rigid requirements about mail, gifts, and visiting times. In spite of this, family members make some effort toward being in touch, hearing each other's news, and being responsive to each other's needs. In the pain and confusion, this often feels quite inadequate on both ends. But people do adapt and adjust.

Many confinements to an institution do end. When one is released and returns to family and community there are new issues to be faced. What were the stresses in the family when the person left? Is there forgiving and "fence mending" that needs to be done? The returning family member also needs to find his or her way into community groups and events. Often this person will feel burdened by the stigma of being institutionalized and not be ready to face others at first. Usually such a one may have obligations to fulfill. These may include outpatient therapy, medications to be taken, or making regular visits to a parole officer. Such families may need loving support to negotiate the changes they have endured.

Reluctant Nursing Home Placement

Other families may face the dilemma of what to do with an elderly member who increasingly is unable to care for him or herself. Perhaps the person is not physically strong enough, or is forgetful, or is not oriented to time and place.

Families have to choose from limited options the best possible care for the person. In such circumstances, it is extremely unlikely there will ever be a return to the family.

Once the decision is taken and placement made, the adjustment for all is again delicate and difficult. A few beloved objects to remind the person of family and home need to be placed where they can be seen and touched. Visits and support need to take place, but also guidance into friendships and activities at the nursing home. It is difficult to overestimate the trauma of the first several weeks for the one placed and for the family. A few are just unable to make the adjustment. Others gradually accept this change as skilled nursing home staffs both meet the needs of their residents and build bridges to those outside, loving and missing their family member.

The Marginally Employed Immigrant

The Diduangleuth family arrived in the U.S. in 1980. They escaped Communist Laos and headed for Thailand, crossing the Mekong River on a homemade raft at night. Not wanting to arouse suspicion, they left all their belongings behind. Once there, they were escorted to a refugee camp along with ten thousand others and waited a year and a half for processing to come to the United States.

Upon arrival at a Midwestern city, they were met by caring members of a church who served as their sponsors. Living in a suburban area of a large city was quite different from life in their village in Laos. Back home, the market, school, and temple were within walking distance of their house. When someone was sick, the "doctor" made a house call. Babies were born at home with the assistance of a midwife. Food was either grown in the backyard or purchased daily at the market. The father, Bounhieng, worked for the government in a nearby office. The mother, Nouphay, was at home during the day taking care of the children and the crops. Relatives lived nearby. This made it easy to have family gatherings, share child care responsibilities, and run errands.

Finding employment in the suburbs of a Midwestern city was not easy because of Bounhieng's lack of a specialized skill, his heavy Lao accent, and the lack of public transportation. When an assembly job was located, about ten miles from his apartment, members of the church drove him to and from work until he was able to obtain a car and driver's license. He began working the "graveyard shift" and slept during the day. Unable to pay the bills on one income, they eventually found work for Nouphay, the wife. This left Donny, a 3-year-old, at home alone with Dad, who slept from eight A.M. to three P.M. Thongsamay, age 10, Vilayvanh, age 13, Somchay, age 16, and

Viengxey, age 17, were all in school five days a week from eight to three thirty. After school, Somchay cared for someone else's children to earn money. Viengxey had a part-time job from four to ten P.M. each day. When Bounhieng, the father, took a second, part-time job from four to ten P.M., the three youngest children were by themselves from three thirty to six thirty, five days a week. When their mother came home, she fixed dinner and went to bed, usually exhausted from being on her feet all day at her job.

The children rarely saw their father during the week and saw their mother only briefly, and in a state of exhaustion. Thirteen-year-old Vilayvanh did a lot of parenting for Thongsamay and Donny.

Weekends consisted of doing laundry, shopping for groceries, cleaning the house, going to church, and helping Lao relatives with any number of things. "Family togetherness" activities were not a part of their experience except on holidays and special occasions. Husband and wife had no opportunities to get away together. They did not go on vacations. In a matter of two years, the way in which they spent each twenty-four-hour period had drastically changed (Wallace 1988).

The Diduangleuth family typifies the tremendous adjustments made and obstacles overcome by numerous families who have immigrated to the United States from Southeast Asia and elsewhere. Their overwhelming success in adjusting in the face of these obstacles is to be applauded. These are families struggling with many space-time issues and are worthy of our sensitive care.

The Firefighter, the Police Officer, the Nurse

Those whose jobs require twenty-four-hour coverage face a different set of issues in regard to family life. Firefighters are often scheduled to be on duty for one full day, twenty-four hours, then off for forty-eight hours. In addition, they may have one other day off each month and an annual vacation. During the twenty-four-hour period on duty, they have a set schedule with specific responsibilities during the day, with free time in the evening for TV, games, or reading, and overnight sleep. Of course, when there is a fire, everything else is suspended to respond to the emergency. But otherwise they cannot leave the premises during their duty. One fire chief called the firehouse a "little prison" and mentioned that some firefighters and their families had a difficult time adjusting to such a schedule early in their career. In addition, many firefighters work a second job on their days off.

Police officers have either rotating shifts, which change frequently, perhaps monthly, or shifts that may change every three months or even annually. There may be different days off each week. Such a system of assignment means many officers must miss programs and events in which their children are involved. A rotating shift and changing days off also make virtually impossible participation in any community events that presuppose availability at a given day or time.

Nurses who are hospital employees also have to contend with changing shifts, often alternating day and night work in the same week. Some find it very hard to adjust easily from sleeping days to sleeping nights within a short time. Some of the costs one endures for working such a schedule are not being able to eat with one's family (or waking up at the "normal" suppertime and trying to eat mashed potatoes and meat loaf), not being able to sleep with one's spouse, and not being in sync with one's own body or with the rest of the world. Such work expectations also interfere with active involvement in church or other community activities.

Persons in each of these occupations spoke of personal and family strain from other sources as well. Police spoke of the danger, the political nature of much of the work, the hostility or apathy of the public with whom they dealt, and the difficulty of shifting from being an enforcement officer to being a family member. Firefighters spoke of the trauma of seeing badly injured persons or folks burned to death, and of the occasional fear of burn, smoke asphyxiation, or other injury to themselves. Nurses mentioned identification with certain patients, the pain of seeing people suffer and sometimes die, the ever-increasing demands upon understaffed hospital personnel. Some persons who render important services to a community do so at significant cost to themselves and to their families.

Fitting Church Response

What all these families have in common are career choices that have placed unusual stress on each of them. This stress may come from schedule, or long absences, or difficult-to-negotiate intervals of presence and absence for key family members.

In order to respond effectively, church leaders have some fresh and creative thinking to do. The central question is, How can we be sensitive and caring toward the people in this part of the spectrum of diverse and changing families?

There are a few things every church can do for the families in their communities with space and time issues.

To begin, church leaders can think through these family issues. Is a commuter family a family? Are the social scientists and the Census Bureau right in saying that having a common dwelling is part of the basic definition of family? Certainly being a family is more a matter of heart and mind than of dwelling place. To be sure, each family member needs to keep all the others informed and be responsive to one another's needs. Long-distance families need to have their own stories and rituals. They may need to learn to work hard at these when they are together—*and* when they are apart. What is going on with the families in military service that belong to our congregation? How do families who have institutionalized members cope in our community? What are the needs of these families?

Further, churches can learn not to lay guilt or shame trips on families with issues of space and time. Instead, they can be accepting of their diverse styles. Rather than condemning commuter families and seeing them as deteriorating, churches can affirm them as pioneers, dealing with a difficult issue. Instead of making nurses or police officers feel guilty that they cannot be faithful choir members, congregations can welcome such persons when they are able to appear.

Churches need to learn not to lay guilt trips on themselves either. Some of these changes mean that persons will be in Sunday worship less often. Faithful church members who were once in worship forty times a year may be fortunate to be able to come twenty-five times a year anymore. The church should not blame itself or its clergy that such changes are occurring in our society. Congregations may want to explore alternative times and styles of Christian education and worship for those with schedule problems.

Again, the church can make an effort to keep in touch with persons. The folks who are away (working, for study, in military service, in temporary assignments) may love being remembered with something as simple as the church newsletter. They may read it much more eagerly than while at home. Military and commuter families may need two copies of the church newspaper sent to separate addresses. Phone contact is often welcomed. A birthday card board can remind church folk of important days in absent members' lives. Small gifts or "care packages" communicate loving care. Audio or video tapes of home church services and activities might be welcome. The military chaplains with whom we spoke emphasized the importance of ongoing contact and support from home churches. If church members have found other temporary church homes when on these assignments, they can be invited to bring back any fresh ideas or programs that they experienced in the other place. The Southern Baptist Sunday School Board has designed a program called "Building Bridges to Adults Away." This plan suggests that a person be appointed to locate, maintain contact with, and mobilize church support for adults away.

Congregations can restructure some of their existing groups (including Sunday church school classes). With erratic schedules, participants may need the chance to be in touch with one another and to have a session that feels rather complete within the alloted time. Flexible support groups for persons with changing schedules might be fitting.

Prayer circles and support for such persons might be appropriate. Interviews with community servants enduring their difficult schedules might communicate appreciation and raise other folks' consciousness. Churches may need to restructure attitudes if they have been indifferent to transient attenders, such as military personnel or university students. Perhaps, because of their brief time in one place and distance from primary groups, they are folks who need loving attention and care the most.

Regarding program ideas for this group of families, such topics as communication, parenting, and stress and conflict management come to mind. Isolated families under great stress may have a problem with spouse or child abuse. A great need might be for seminars on attitudes toward time and management of time. Perhaps, in the light of our situation, we need fresh thinking, so that we can pray with the psalmist, "So teach us to number our days [and our hours and our minutes] that we may get a heart of wisdom"! (Ps. 90:12).

Resources and References

About Deployment. 1985. South Deerfield, Mass.: Channing L. Bete Co.

D'Orso, Mike. 1988. "Navy Wives." *Tidewater Living*, Feb. 7, pp. 1–7; Feb. 8, pp. 1–3; Feb. 9, p. 2.

Gerstel, Naomi, and Harriet Engel Gross. 1982. "Commuter Marriages: A Review." In Harriet Gross and Marvin B. Sussman, eds., *Alternatives to Traditional Family Living. Marriage and Family Review,* vol. 5, no. 2 (Summer), pp. 71–94. New York: Sage Publications.

––––––. 1983. "Commuter Marriage: Couples Who Live Apart." In Eleanor D. Macklin and Roger H. Rubin, eds., *Contemporary Families and Alternative Lifestyles.* Beverly Hills, Calif.: Sage Publications.

––––––. 1984. *Commuter Marriage.* New York: Guildford Press.

Halley, Michael D., CDR, CHC, USN, Command Chaplain, USS *Coral Sea,* personal correspondence.

Hunter, Edna Jo. 1982. *Families Under the Flag: A Review of Military Family Literature.* New York: Praeger Publishers.

––––––. 1986. "The Marine Corps Family: Looking Backward, Going Forward." *Marine Corps Gazette,* March, pp. 60–63.

––––––, and D. Stephen Nice, eds. 1978. *Military Families: Adaptation to Change.* New York: Praeger Publishers.

Kersey, Katharine, and Janet Schwenke. 1982. "Military Daddy: Now You See Him, Now You Don't." *Ladycom,* June, pp. 65–67.

Logan, Kathleen Vestal. 1987. "The Emotional Cycle of Deployment." *Proceedings*, February, pp. 43–47.

Wade, Ruth Ann. Undated. "Building Bridges to Adults Away." Nashville: Sunday School Board of The Southern Baptist Convention (pamphlet)

Wallace, Sherry. 1988. Personal correspondence.

Winfield, Fairlee E. 1985. *Commuter Marriage: Living Together Apart*. New York: Columbia University Press.

York, Nancy K. 1978. "The Legal Struggle for a Military Woman's Right to Have Children." In Edna J. Hunter and D. Stephen Nice, eds., *Military Families: Adaptation to Change*. New York: Praeger Publishers.

8

Families with Members Who Have Disabilities

Congregations need to rethink their ministry with and to families that have members with disabilities in light of two important arenas of change: the transformations in family life we have documented in the preceding chapters and the revolution in self-perception held by families that have members with disabilities.

Households that include persons with disabilities are caught up in the same powerful social forces that affect all other families. Five are important enough to restate here. First is a longer life span, especially for women. Second is the massive move of women into the paid labor force. This is linked to a third change, from a manufacturing economy to one based on service industries, information processing, and financial management. Fourth, technology puts ever more control over life-and-death decisions for individuals and for the whole human species in our own hands. Fifth, a new sense of self-esteem and a new willingness to assert themselves has arisen among traditionally disfranchised groups. Families living with members who have disabilities are participants in all of these changing patterns.

We believe, however, that the liberation movement among people with disabilities has made the most difference to their families. As these families have shared in this movement, their sights have risen. They have come to have higher expectations of themselves as families and higher expectations of the community. The self-understanding and self-acceptance, especially of parents with disabled children, has changed and is changing for the better. Let's explore this transformation in self-understanding. It has enormous implications for the church's family ministries.

A major contributor to the more positive self-images held by these parents is the availability of educational programs for their children. Their twenty-five-year effort to open school systems to all children succeeded with the passage of Public Law 94-142 in 1975. This law mandated the education of all children, regardless of impairment. This changed the social and legal status of families with disabled children. Efforts to dismantle the law during the Reagan administration were effectively resisted. Families now expect that their children with disabilities will have appropriate schooling. Added to this is recent federal legislation encouraging states to begin or expand early intervention services for children likely to have disabilities. Facing up to the special child's needs at an early age is easier when helpful programs are available.

These changes in law and public policy have changed the ways families with seriously impaired children see themselves and their children. They no longer feel like supplicants before a bureaucracy with no accountability for the decisions it makes. Rather, families feel entitled to ask for appropriate services. Such self-confidence replaces the impulse to hide an impaired child and withdraw from community life. It reduces the urge to search endlessly for a "cure," or to surrender one's child to an institution the moment one's physician suggests it.

Recently, Marsha Ann Hoffman-Williamson studied the daily life of three families who had both a child with Down's syndrome and typical children. She uncovered a pattern of family living hard to distinguish from surrounding neighbors with no special-needs children. "An important assumption made by all the family members is that their identity as a family takes precedent [sic] over their identification as a family with a retarded child" (Hoffman-Williamson 1984, p. 2). Families of persons with disabilities have come to expect something approaching the lifestyle of typical families.

Conversation with families who have children labeled autistic has revealed an expectation that community help will be forthcoming. One mother who discovered a county-funded respite care service said, "I grab whatever is out there. I look for anything that Davey can be signed up for. If it's there, I grab it." In the school-based parents' group this mother attends, information about what is available and from whom is routinely exchanged. There is no longer the attitude that a family who seeks or needs help from the community is somehow a failure, challenging a basic American myth of the self-sufficient and independent family. Parents of this generation's disabled children expect help from their communities.

What Are "Disabilities"
and How Many Families Are Involved?

The term "disability" refers to the special challenge facing persons who have physical or mental impairments. Some impairments are quite specific and require a person to make specific special adaptations. Examples are blindness, deafness, juvenile diabetes, occasional seizures, reading problems, or a damaged limb. Other impairments are more general and interfere with many aspects of a person's function in daily life. Examples are mental retardation, emotional disturbance, spina bifida, cerebral palsy, autism, or severe learning disabilities. Because these latter delay or disrupt normal developmental patterns in children and adolescents, they are often called developmental disabilities. Any condition that seriously impairs the emotional, intellectual, or social development of a child can be considered a developmental disability. Most disabilities arise from damage to the developing fetus and especially to the central nervous system prior to or at birth. Of course, accident or disease at any point can leave a person with a permanent disability.

How many families include members with disabilities? No one takes a census of families with disabled members. But one can construct an estimate of how many families live with disabilities by reviewing the counts that are taken by different parts of the government serving persons with special needs. The information shared here comes from the *Statistical Abstract of the United States: 1988*, 108th Edition, which is the most recent available at this writing. As of 1986 there were 4,317,000 children in special education; 2,225,000 disabled veterans receiving benefits; 146,000 adults and children in intermediate-care facilities for persons with retardation; 354,000 adults and some institutionalized children receiving Supplemental Security Income; 131,000 former miners receiving black-lung disease benefits; and (as of March 1987) 13,350,000 former workers receiving disability income. These figures do not include persons living in nursing homes, state institutions, or community living arrangements (group homes) for those with mental impairments or disturbances or physical disabilities. A conservative estimate of the number of persons with disabilities is 10 percent of the U.S. population, or about 24,000,000 people (based on the 1987 estimate of U.S. population of 241,519,000). Clearly, many families are affected, perhaps as many as 20 percent.

Think about your congregation. Try to name the households in which someone is coping with physical disabilities or chronic illness or permanent injuries, caring for a frail elderly relative, concerned about a family member with long-standing psychiatric problems, or raising a child with developmental disabilities. How many can you identify in your congregation? In the two-hundred-member congregation where one of us belongs, there are twenty-one households in which someone has a disability.

Family Issues

When Disability Occurs

What are the issues facing these families? We will discuss five family issues: when the disability occurs, the emotional response, the theological response, the family's task, and support strategies. When the disability occurs or is discovered makes an enormous difference. If at birth, or in early childhood, then parents must come to grips with a host of decisions about medical treatment and/or early-intervention programs while coping with intense feelings of losing their dreams for this child. Today's technology makes possible the survival of seriously damaged newborns and parents find themselves confronted with terrible decisions about whether to authorize medical procedures that assure physical survival of infants with enormous long-term needs for special therapies and education.

If the newborn or young child is firstborn, and the parents relatively inexperienced, they may have a harder time recognizing their child's impairments and the implications for their role as parents. Uncertainty and a lack of self-confidence are acute. All parents with an impaired young child need solid information about the disability they confront and assurance that they are competent to deal with it. The single most effective source for both is often other parents who have faced the same crisis.

When disability takes place in adolescence or young adulthood, parents have a different role. Typically the source of disability in these years is an accident leading to head or spinal cord injury. The youngster will need to be part of the decision-making about treatment, therapy, or special education insofar as possible. Living arrangements, vocational issues, and redeveloping self-esteem come to the fore. Critical to all these is maintaining a focus on ability rather than on disability, on what is or can be possible, on what can be achieved.

As children with disabilities mature, new questions face their parents: Who will "stand guard" alongside these vulnerable adults when parents are gone? Where will they live? What will occupy their talents? Will they have friends? Special education in most states is available until one reaches twenty-one years. Services for adults of whatever disability are generally lacking. This represents the next great challenge to the disability advocacy movement.

Increasingly, the family member with a disability is an aging parent or grandparent. A recent survey indicated that 25 percent of all workers are caring for an elderly family member living with them or nearby (Edwards and Snyder 1987). With advanced age comes physical decline and sometimes serious physical or mental impairments. Families face decisions about when and if to use nursing home facilities. Those caring for an elderly relative in their own home need to be relieved from time to time. Understandings need to be reached about how to deal with possible final illness. How will decisions be made if the elderly member loses the ability to make his or her own decisions? Will heroic measures be taken to prolong life? Is there to be a living will?

Finally, since a significant number of adult workers receive disability payments, some children must live with a parent who becomes disabled. The implications of this fact are enormous for family income and role reversals between parent and child. A family may need to revise daily routines, reassign household work, and perhaps remodel its dwelling. Friends, relatives, and substitute caretakers are crucial for the one undergoing rehabilitation or retraining and for the spouse adjusting to extra demands. When the disability involves head injury, there may be shifts in personality, decreases in cognitive function, and memory loss. If the spinal cord is injured, the spouses' sexual relationship may be disrupted. A good rehabilitation program for the injured partner will include attention to sexual functioning. Both partners will need to be taught new ways to handle this critical aspect of their relationship.

Emotional Response

The second major issue faced by these families is their emotional response to their situation. When a disability is first identified, feelings of shock and grief, guilt and anxiety, anger and fatigue are sure to follow. A major impairment of a family member is likely to provoke a grief reaction among other family members. Grief reactions usually include times of denial, anger, depression, and bargaining.

Denying the full extent of an impairment, or even its reality, is a safety mechanism. Denial cushions the shock of what has happened or been named for the first time. It gives the mind time to absorb the impact of a traumatic reality. Denial that persists, however, blocks adaptive responses. Long after the mother, usually the primary caretaker, accepts that her child has special needs, the father may still be in denial. Fathers will often withdraw from the family into work, where things may not be so unpredictable or saddening. When this pattern occurs, the couple relationship is strained.

Disability can also bring with it guilt and anxiety. Every parent sometimes asks, when something untoward happens with a child, "What did I do wrong?" Discovering a developmental disability in one's young child, confronting an adolescent injured in an accident, or even having to care for one's aging parent with Alzheimer's disease evokes that guilty question. Self-blame can lead to blaming one's spouse or doctor or other helper. If only one's partner was doing or not doing something, the problem would go away! The feeling of blame is always painfully disruptive of family relationships; no other family so needs to feel acceptance within itself as the family that has a member with a disability.

With guilt comes anxiety that one cannot cope, that there is no way of living with the fact of disability, that the situation is hopeless. Uncertainty about the future of the one with disabilities, fear of social rejection, and embarrassment in public situations may be intense and lead to times of depression. Knowing the facts about an impairment may reassure; but the presence of other families facing the same or similar situation and caring dialogue with them will bring the most lasting and powerful reduction of anxiety in families coping with a disabled member.

The other side of anxiety and depression may well be anger. One's anger may find many targets: the disabled one, the self, medical professionals, the social service system, an apathetic public, God. A challenge for family members is to recognize their anger, deal with it openly, and avoid aiming the anger at each other. Anger can spark creative responses and energize solid, long-term work to find or invent means of help. Anger can sustain the struggle to secure services, pass appropriate legislation, focus public attention, and challenge service providers to improve and extend their help.

A number of writers (Featherstone 1980; Gargiulo 1985; Murphy 1981) have drawn a parallel between the stages of grief outlined by Kübler-Ross in her studies of dying people and similar stages parents of children with disabilities are said to go through. Given the experience of one of the authors of this book as a parent of two children with severe disabilities, and in our work with other parents, we find the perspective of Robert Perske more helpful: "Some experts have described in detail the stages you are expected to face. The only trouble is that parents who are adjusting to children with handicaps do not follow a set course. Each parent reacts differently" (Perske 1981, p. 11).

A serious limitation of the "stages of grief" perspective is that it overlooks the efforts families make to create something out of their situation. It sees only grief when also there are sometimes pride in an accomplishment and satisfaction with an advocacy job well done. There is even enjoyment of the incongruity that occurs when one's child responds inappropriately. One parent tells with amusement how his autistic son, known for memorizing and repeating commercial slogans, answered a lifeguard's reprimand with a smile and "There's more for your life at Sears!"

Perske offers a simple list of experiences parents may or may not have as they raise a child with disabilities. *The drags.* At times one may feel so tired one just drags around. The temptation to withdraw will be overwhelming. Perske suggests some time out is probably healthy, as long as one comes back into the struggle after the respite. *The speeds.* This feels as if one's spring is wound too tightly, and in a frenzy of activity one tackles everything at once. One seeks to get at the task even if some motion is wasted. *The blocks.* Bad news comes, but the ears refuse to hear and the eyes refuse to see the evidence. The mind blocks out what it cannot deal with. The transition from superbaby or superchild to one with an impairment cannot be made all at once. Making the shift slowly is appropriate, provided the shift is made. *The hurts.* Sleepless nights, feeling nervous and edgy, crying, feeling deeply pained is part of confronting a disability. Sometimes people gain strength from enduring such pain. Companionship may be a key to enduring it. *The guilts.* Some parents will feel that they have sinned against God in an extraordinary way to have caused the disability of a family member. Perske says this is a phony guilt—it is not the same kind one feels when caught by self or others in a real transgression. He counsels encouraging persons to move on. Ruminating on one's past simply blocks one's adjustment to the real situation that must be faced. *The greats.* There will come days when a parent feels that he or she is the greatest mom or dad living to be coping so well with such a challenging situation! Some parents may even feel that God has chosen them to bear a special burden in recognition of their superior quality. Of course, the feeling won't last, and there is danger of falling into the guilts again. A balanced perspective on one's parenting, its strengths and weaknesses, is desirable. *The hates.* Hurting so deeply can lead to blaming, and almost anyone can become a target. Someone will say or do something to "justify" unleashing one's whole load of anger. Feeling anger and hatred is normal. Acting on it may be costly. Hurting others tends to make one hurt also, and the cycle of hurt is reinforced. *The escapes.* There may be times of wanting to walk out the door and not come back, or to close one's eyes and never open them again. One may be ashamed of such impulses, though many parents with disabled children admit to them. They too will pass. Perske advises parents to hang on.

Is there a time of acceptance? Is a disabling condition ever "acceptable"? Do families with members who have disabilities come to an equilibrium of feeling and an even keel in their functioning? Each stage in the life of such a family poses new challenges and problems. The old feelings of grief and fatigue can and do reemerge as these are met. But at the same time, families draw encouragement from their past experience of meeting challenges. Key ingredients to reaching a kind of working equilibrium are: finding answers to theological questions, dealing with the tasks of family life, and creating or finding a support network.

Theological Response

The bewildering feelings and experiences known by family members coping with disabilities raise theological questions. Responding theologically is the third major issue facing these families. Indeed, the single greatest service the church can offer families is an opportunity to raise and grapple with theological issues involved in disability. The first question one is inclined to raise is, How can this have happened to me? One parent has answered the question, Why me? with another: Who else? Her point is that family pain by any other name is still family pain. The stress of being in a family where someone has a disability is not quantitatively different from the stress another family faces because someone in it has alcoholism or abuses drugs, is alienated or in jail. "We do not love more—or hurt more—because our sorrow springs from a different well" (Akerley 1984, p. 88).

A more theologically meaningful question is, "Since we are a family with a disabled member, what in God's name are we to make of this situation? What is God calling us to do with it? How is God with us in it?" This vocational question leads to a central theological issue that arises in any tragic circumstance: How can a just and loving all-powerful God contrive the creation of people with disabilities? Or permit the crippling traffic accident? Or consent to the carnage of war? Traditionally, the faithful are counseled to affirm that God wills all things and that the omnipotent and just ways of the Almighty are beyond finding out.

Burton Cooper's suggestion in his provocative book, *Why, God?* however, seems to us both intriguing and fruitful for constructing a theology of tragedy. Cooper acknowledges what he calls the "monarchical image of God" to be the main theme of traditional theology. Yet it is not the only biblical possibility for understanding who God is and how God acts. Cooper points out, "We have a tendency, sometimes, to think of Scripture as if it were a train on a single track heading determinedly for its final destination. But the Bible is not really like that. Perhaps the Bible is more like a deep coal mine with many seams. . . . If we think of the Bible as a coal mine with seams we have been mining for centuries and others we have hardly touched, then we have our clue to how a view of God other than that of the main theological tradition can also be a biblical view" (Cooper 1988, p. 45).

The traditional image portrays God as "great, awesomely mysterious and powerful. . . . All-controlling and all knowing, nothing happens outside his will. He never changes in any way; he is eternally the same. He especially never changes his mind" (ibid.). Nevertheless, there is another biblical image, richly attested if we but look with fresh eyes at Scripture. It is the image of the vulnerable God. Cooper draws our attention to less exploited seams in the biblical mine. He lifts up the tone of passion in God's anguishing over Israel (Jer. 4:19; 31:20; Mic. 6:3; Hos. 11:8–9). He notes God's wrathful passion toward Israel's waywardness (Isa. 33:1), echoed in Jesus' words to the scribes, Pharisees, the Temple money changers and trinket sellers (Matt. 23:27–28 and 21:13). God is vulnerable to the deeds and words of human beings. The Creator's creatures matter to the Holy One. Think of the lament and metaphor of motherly love on the lips of Jesus in Matthew 23:37.

These texts are just a sampling that evokes a different image of God. This God is not the all-controlling and all-knowing king. Not an impassive judge who can calmly mete out a sinner's due. Not a tester of righteousness who subjects the faithful to trial. Rather this God is caught in the conflict of love and justice. This God feels the conflict in the depths of the divine heart. God is vulnerable to suffering because God feels the competing claims of love and justice. "God suffers from those who perpetuate injustice (the treacherous ones, the destroyers) as, analogously—but only analogously—a music lover suffers upon hearing music played off-key. God suffers with the victims of injustice as a loving wife suffers when her husband bears undeserved affliction. And God suffers with the punishment of the unjust as a loving father suffers even when his children are only getting their just deserts" (Cooper 1988, p. 50).

But, if God suffers, then God is in some sense self-limited. Divine power is not absolute in all respects. Great evils can be done by human beings without God's permission. Great plagues and natural catastrophes can wreak suffering without specific order from the cosmic throne. Genetic anomalies, birth defects, and accidents can befall persons without divine sanction. One need not blame God for the bad things that happen to good people (Kushner 1981).

To those conditioned by the monarchical image of God, the concept of a vulnerable God with limits is startling and to some deeply dissatisfying. A universe of such freedom that events occur outside God's plan and order is perceived by some as a universe of chaos. One's sense of security is threatened. But does the doctrine of God the unlimited monarch reflect human security needs or divine reality? Does it arise simply out of revelation, or is it also in part an expression of the human political imagination? Does the classical image of God as impassive, only active, never receptive, and unlimited in power betray our patriarchal traditions as much as biblical traditions? Totalitarian power is ultimately an evil on the human scene. Coerced obedience and loyalty are not obedience and loyalty at all. Is it not odd, then, to attribute coercion to the Deity and worship it?

But if "force is no attribute of God" (the Epistle to Diognetus quoted in McGill 1982, p. 82), what, then, is the nature of divine power? Arthur McGill helps us to an alternate understanding of divine power, the holy power of self-giving service. McGill draws on the insights of the early Trinitarian theologian Athanasius, and on a careful analysis of the ministry of Jesus the Christ. He focuses our attention on the way God in Christ responds to human need. It is a way unlike earthly rulers, the Gentile lords, who demand submission through their power to coerce needy subjects with violence. God's powerfulness in the face of human need is revealed and vindicated in a completely opposite way. "It does not dominate, threaten, or impose violence; it *serves*" (McGill 1982, p. 62). So Jesus ministers to the poor and rarely to the rich, to the sinful and rarely to the righteous, to the weak and rarely to the strong, to those who are dying rather than those who are full of life. It is precisely in our need and vulnerability that God's power of service is effective. Poor people are fed, sinners forgiven, weak ones strengthened, and even the dead made alive.

God's limits are the limits of love that seeks but does not coerce communion. They are the limits required of a creator of freedom. They are the limits of one who serves rather than terrifies creatures in their neediness and suffering. God's power is the power of redemption and meaning-making. So we affirm that God does not send disability to test a family's faith or improve its character. Yet we also affirm that by God's grace a family's faith and character may be strengthened as they struggle to cope. God does not ordain disability in one person so that others may learn what is really important in life. Yet, through God's grace, facing the challenge of disability can redirect family priorities beyond the manic consumerism of American life. God does not permit disabilities in order to teach spiritual lessons, or expose social evil, or make a place for miracles. Yet through God's grace, spiritual truths will be learned in the presence of human vulnerability; disability advocates will arise to challenge evil; and caring medical and educational personnel will work all manner of miracles. Through God's power of service and self-giving, families whose members have disabilities will experience redeeming moments in their struggle. They will discover working answers to their deepest questions.

Family Task

The fourth issue confronting families with disabled members is to complete their task as a family. In this they face the same challenge as other families. All families of whatever sort are expected in all cultures to fulfill the functions assigned to them by their culture. All societies have a theory of child development, usually implicit and unconscious. There are prescribed goals for family life and a script to follow in achieving those goals. Usually the system works well. Parents and society are organized by the theory, so they support each other in the task of raising a competent next generation. A brief examination of the cultural script for parenting in American society will clarify this point.

American families look to the writers of child care books, to psychology and social science, and sometimes to media figures, rather than to religious or traditional leaders for direction about raising children. Currently, the goals and functions of family life are likely to be expressed in terms of "family strengths" (Stinnett 1984) or "family health" (Curran 1985). Lewis offers this definition of a healthy family: "The term 'healthy' refers to families that do the two important jobs of the family well. They stabilize or promote growth in the parent's [sic] personalities, and raise children who achieve high levels of individuality and autonomy" (1979, p. 10. See also Lewis et al. 1976).

Lewis, a psychiatrist, studied relatively affluent, white families that seemed to be functioning well, using all the latest tools of psychiatric evaluation. In a subsequent project Lewis added African-American social scientists to his team and researched a group of working class black families (Lewis and Looney 1983). That research confirmed the earlier findings except that families below a certain threshold of income uniformly seemed to be functioning badly.

What is important about this definition of healthy families, however, is its congruence with general American ideology. Note the language of industry (families do two important "jobs"), the emphasis on growth, the focus on individuality and autonomy. Healthy families are productive, enterprising units turning out mental health and high achievers of self-fulfillment, self-direction, and self-sufficiency. There is nothing remarkable about this statement at all. One can find it echoed in all the popular child care books, advice columns, and in most texts on the family and pastoral theology.

Parents meet the goal of producing children who grow up to be autonomous adults by following a "cultural script." The American cultural script for parenting is a developmental one. It calls for children to meet specified milestones by certain target ages. Parents are well aware of these milestones. Who has not heard a parent brag that his or her child walked or talked earlier than is typical? or worry aloud about whether wanting designer jeans at age 5 might be a little soon for such consumerism? or fret over the 18-year-old who is not dating yet? As each milestone is passed, parents are reassured that their offspring is achieving the prescribed independence and autonomy expected in our culture.

Of course families are not alone in carrying out these prescriptions. The cultural script organizes social institutions as well as families. Thus as one's child reaches a particular stage of development, complementary social organizations are there to meet the family. For preschoolers there are nursery schools. For school-age children there are after-school sports or music lessons or Bible clubs. For older children and youth there are scout troops, summer camps, church youth groups, and the like. Families and the institutions of society are helped to function together by the cultural script for family life.

But what happens if this script is violated? Families experience stress precisely where the correlation between social organization and family developmental stage breaks down. Perhaps the most glaring example of such breakdown today is the unmet need for day care. The cultural script for families does not yet envision two working parents with young children. Family reality has outrun cultural norms. Social organizations are scrambling to organize themselves in terms of a new script for a new (formerly "deviant"!) family.

Understanding how families and society are organized by a cultural script helps us see why families with disabled members often experience stress. Because their children do not meet developmental milestones as prescribed, these families often find themselves out of phase with social organizations. Their children do not fit into day care centers or teams or choirs without some adjustment on the part of the institution. Often the needed organizational partner is simply not there. These families have to work hard to make up for missing social partners. Indeed much of the energy powering parent advocacy and self-advocacy disability groups springs from a growing recognition that families must have the support of social institutions in order to function. Consequently, social institutions must be restructured to respond to the realities of changing families.

Creating or Finding Support

Often the social organizations that provide support and help to most families are closed to families with special needs. These families must put much effort into creating a support system on their own. In work with four families who have children with autism, one of the authors of this book explored the strategies they used to create and find support. As one might expect, these families depended on kin, older siblings, neighbors, and friends for assistance. But in addition, all four families turned to what can be called "formal friends" for help. These individuals were paid for their support, but were often more than simply employees. The housekeeper in one family was the intimate confidant of the mother, a professional in her work. Their mutual caring and respect was deep. In another family, the mother recruited a friend as a respite care worker. She then encouraged her friend to become certified and paid by the county mental health–mental retardation system! Two of the families also paid teachers from their children's special school for weekend care. This gave the parents, and sometimes their other children, needed time off. The use of such formal friends prompts a question. What implications are there here for church ministry with families who have special needs for respite care?

The other notable family support strategy these four families pursued was membership in a variety of voluntary organizations. For the most part, these were related directly to the needs of their children with disabilities. One family, however, belonged to a hockey association for which their two older sons played. Interestingly, other parents in the association were well aware of the family's special-needs child. They commented on his progress, on how well the parents coped, and the like. They too were part of the family's support system.

Two of the families were committed participants in local churches. One Protestant family told a story with some positive elements to it but in a not very positive framework. They explained that their youngster attends with the fours and fives, which is his age group. There is a woman who works with him alone, something like an aide, in the classroom. She is recruited along with other preschool workers. During church service, their son is excluded from the nursery and is by himself with another volunteer. The mother commented unhappily about her son's exclusion from the nursery: "Other parents complained." Her husband interrupted, "I can understand." The mother continued, "The concern about him hurting another is understandable; he throws things. Sometimes the teachers don't know how to handle him." But then the father volunteered criticism of the church for being slow to respond to the needs of his family. He related this slow response to a general lack of openness to special needs. "My wife," he said, "worked for seventeen years on the Fresh Air Fund [bringing city children to the country for a summer vacation] and the poorest response always came from the churches."

What Is Expected of the Churches?

Having identified the issues confronted by families whose members have disabilities, we can explore the responses of the churches, both actual and potential. We can identify what is needed and how congregations can be effective ministers to, with, and for these families. One thing that is clear from listening to parents: Families increasingly *expect* their religious communities to respond and respond to their specific needs!

Listen to what a Jewish mother said: "The Jewish Federation has some programs for the blind and the hearing-impaired; nothing for MR [mentally retarded] or SED [socially and emotionally disturbed]. I wish they'd make some effort." This mother described how she and two friends went to a budget hearing of the Jewish Federation and asked for programs for their children. There is Bar Mitzvah preparation for learning disabled youngsters, she told me, but not for her child with autism. There is no program for her son during Sabbath services. She commented: "I've lost my faith in organized religion, but not in God."

In a parents' support group one mother told another, "Your priest is supposed to know where the nearest special CCD class [Confraternity of Christian Doctrine, a catechism class] is for your child. Let me give you the number at the archdiocese where he can call and find out. It's his job to know that and get your kid enrolled." A Protestant family changed churches in part because the young assistant pastor of the new church encouraged the whole family to attend together. This meant both parents and both children, including the one with developmental disabilities. Formerly Mother and Dad took turns attending, believing that their disabled child was not happy in the church nor particularly welcome. Families expect their religious communities to respond, and when the response is slow or lacking, there is disappointment, anger, and sometimes a decision to drop out.

Family Needs and Church Responses

Emotional Support

The first needs a family has when its issue is a member with a disability are information and emotional support. Their pastor may be the first one called, and in some cases the pastor may be the only resource in the community. Knowing who else to call, where in the county or city human service system to look for help, is important information for pastors and congregational leaders to have. Responding with informed caring can make all the difference to a family facing the news of a disability.

Inclusion

Second, families coping with a disability need to be included. Given the movement from automatic institutionalization of people with severe impairments toward community-based education, work opportunities, and care, churches need to refocus their response. Historically churches have responded to special-needs persons in a highly segregated way, providing special church school classes or residential programs. Rarely has the church focused on ministering with the family and the person who has disabilities as a part of its regular program.

Families who live with disabilities want to participate. They are looking for ways to include their family member with special needs in the life of the faith community. Can the church school mainstream their youngster into the regular group with the extra help of an aide? Can the congregation provide sensitive emotional support? Is there a way that both parents can attend services at the same time when that is the normal expectation? Will the church be a partner in advocacy for inclusion in the wider community?

What has been learned in the last decades about ministering with the whole family unit through family enrichment activities applies to ministry with families who have a disabled member. Marriage enrichment retreats, parenting classes, family camping, family night programs, and family clusters (a family cluster is a group of four to six household units learning together intergenerationally with a trained leader, focusing on the concerns that animate the particular group) are certainly helpful and valid ministries to families who live with disabilities. Family camping and family clusters are the most responsive to these family units. They offer the most potential for including such families in activities that are enjoyed by all families.

We would say a qualified "yes" to community ecumenical or interfaith church school classes for special needs persons, but we would also ask what about integrating children and youth with special needs into the regular church education program? If participation in worship is not possible for an individual, can a place be found for that one to be present, in the building, doing something appropriate and experiencing such interaction as is feasible? (Perhaps some of our worship services would benefit from participants who are a little less inhibited, a little less reluctant to indicate when the experience is genuinely engaging and when it is boring and irrelevant!)

The intergenerational approach to religious education can be a rich experience of both sharing and learning for all persons and lends itself to inclusion of those with special needs. In a family cluster or intergenerational class there is a wider range of things to do and often more to do that is not tied into strictly cognitive modes of learning and responding.

Family Support

A third area of need and response is that of family support. Support groups for parents of children with impairments do exist under religious auspices here and there. Churches are among the more hospitable places where support groups can get started. If you are in a community with little in the way of services for families with members who have disabilities, then your mission is clear. Take the initiative to help create the family support and advocacy group that is going to reform your community! Do not overlook the need of siblings for support. A social gathering as a support experience for sisters and brothers of those with impairments can be crucial. These are the family members most often shortchanged as parents focus on the urgent needs of their impaired youngster.

While support groups are important, respite care is even more important (Holpern 1980, Parker 1980, and Kolb 1981). Families need relief from the often unrelenting needs of an impaired family member. Time off from sometimes constant care so that the couple or family can do some typical family things together can reenergize a sagging family system. This goes for families caring for a frail elderly relative as much as for those with a developmentally disabled child. *Sharing Care: The Christian Ministry of Respite Care* (Murphy 1986) outlines the practical steps congregations can take to provide this support service to families. Congregations can provide a quality of care that is hardly ever available, at any price: the presence of care givers who know a family well and are trusted friends.

Another important form of support is the kind that mission support groups or lay ministry groups offer their members. Families of persons who are disabled often find themselves up to their eyebrows in voluntary association activity, advocating for their disability group. Energy runs low. Burnout is never far away. To be supported by a group that values what one is doing, and appreciates the social justice mandates behind it, is an irreplaceable resource. The mission of the faith community is in fact carried by its lay members in the places of their employment and voluntary activity. Lay ministry support groups are critical to maintaining that witness and they are vital to those in mission on behalf of persons with special needs.

Perhaps no institution or group has more potential than the church for supporting families of persons with special needs when they ask the ultimate question: Who will care for our vulnerable family member when we are not here? One of the most significant conceptual and practical advances in answering this question is the emergence of the "support circle" (Forest and Snow 1987). A support circle is a group of friends who covenant to surround a person who has special needs and vulnerabilities. They covenant to be for that person companions, advocates, planners, monitors, and caretakers. Support circles are "for life." That means that while the members may change, the group will be there for the person with disabilities. Family members are members of the circle as long as they are able and it seems appropriate. The concept is a "natural" for a congregation seeking to be supportive of families who have members with disabilities. *Supportive Care in the Congregation* (Preheim-Bartel and Neufeldt 1986) is a slim manual outlining how support circles work and how they can be created in a congregation.

Advocacy

Finally, we want to lift up advocacy as another family support strategy. Advocacy takes many forms. One form is consciousness-raising. There is no body with more potential than the religious community for consciousness-raising about the needs and gifts of persons living with disabilities. The challenge is to keep the issue alive on the religious community's agenda. Obviously the environmental crisis, the possibility of a nuclear holocaust, and the madness of current United States policy in Central America, not to mention South Africa, require constant attention and effort. But families whose members are living with disabilities are entitled to their place on the church agenda as well. Harold Wilke and the Caring Congregation organization (Wilke 1980) are teaching us some things about consciousness-raising. The annual "accessible Sabbath" they promote and resource is being observed increasingly. Their newsletter, *The Healing Community*, regularly tells the stories of congregations who are becoming accessible, welcoming places for persons who have disabilities and their families.

A second form of advocacy is helping to shape public policy. Increasingly issues faced by individual families are becoming matters of public policy. Private tragedies and dilemmas are debated daily in the press and in legislative halls. For example, since the availability of legal abortion, couples or potential parents are choosing whether or not to carry to term a fetus with detectable impairments. With the development of medical technology, families, physicians, and hospitals are facing difficult choices about whether or not to treat life-threatening conditions in severely or even not so severely impaired newborns. What shall be the public policy? Surely the ethical reflection of the churches is relevant to these public questions.

Another form of advocacy is prophetic witness and action. In the faith community the prophet is honored, and prophetic witness to those in the seats of power is at the heart of our Judeo-Christian heritage. Speaking out alongside persons with disabilities for the justice due them is critical. Joining with disability advocacy groups around specific issues is certainly appropriate for any concerned congregation.

At the same time, the family that nurtures the prophet is also honored in our tradition. A familial advocacy of one-to-one caring is at the heart of our faith as well. The nuclear arms race requires one kind of advocacy. Including families living with disabilities in church and community requires another. Both are essential. It seems to us that the one-to-one advocacy of friends caring for each other and relating each other to wider circles of friendly support and interest is central to what it means to be included in a religious community. It is this kind of advocacy, this kind of ministry on behalf of families who have members with disabilities, that we hope to see more of in the church.

Finally, a local church vignette. Two pastors of a Midwestern small town congregation found themselves ministering with two young adult men who had become paralyzed. After their hospitalization, the men wanted to attend church. The pastors advocated for ramps, which the congregation reluctantly erected. To everyone's surprise, the ramps drew others with similar needs to the congregation. Soon the staff of a nearby group home for adults with retardation asked if their clients could attend that church. Responding positively with an invitation to worship, the congregation discovered a need for a new adult class. The families of these adults responded with gratitude and receptivity for further ministry. The pastors said this unfolding of ministry did not stem from any special vision or initiative on their part. The church simply responded to the needs that were put before them. Isn't that the way ministry grows?

Resources and References

Akerley, Mary S. 1984. "Developmental Changes in Families with Autistic Children: A Parent's Perspective." In Eric Schopler and Gary B. Mesibov, eds., *The Effects of Autism on the Family.* New York: Plenum Press.

Cooper, Burton Z. 1988. *Why, God?* Atlanta: John Knox Press.

Curran, Dolores. 1985. *Stress and the Healthy Family.* Minneapolis: Winston-Seabury.

Edwards, Gregg, and David Snyder. 1987. "Families and the Future:

Sustaining the Social Base of Our Economic Enterprise." Special Public Policy Section, *National Council on Family Relations Newsletter*, December, pp. 1–4.

Featherstone, Helen. 1980. *A Difference in the Family: Life with a Disabled Child*. New York: Basic Books.

Forest, Marsha, and Judith Snow. 1987. "The Joshua Committee: An Advocacy Model." In *A Story That I Heard*, collected by David B. Schwartz, John McKnight, and Michael Kendrick. Harrisburg, Pa.: Developmental Disabilities Planning Council, pp. 48–54.

Gargiulo, Richard M. 1985. *Working with Parents of Exceptional Children: A Guide for Professionals*. Boston: Houghton Mifflin Co.

Hoffman-Williamson, Marsha A. 1984. "Three Down's Syndrome Children and Their Siblings." Doctoral dissertation, University of Pennsylvania.

Holpern, Peggy I. 1980. "Home-based Respite Care and Family Regenerative Power in Families with a Retarded Child." Doctoral dissertation, University of Maryland.

Ikeler, Bernard. 1986. *Parenting Your Disabled Child*. Philadelphia: Westminster Press.

Kolb, Cynthia L. 1981. "The Effectiveness of a Structured Group Experience on a Mother's Adjustment to a Handicapped Child." Doctoral dissertation, Kent State University.

Kushner, Harold. 1981. *When Bad Things Happen to Good People*. New York: Schocken Books.

Leonard, Joe H. 1986. "Families and Autism." Doctoral dissertation, Columbia University Teachers College.

Lewis, Jerry M. 1979. *How's Your Family? A Guide to Identifying Your Family's Strengths and Weaknesses*. New York: Brunner/Mazel.

————, et al. 1976. *No Single Thread: Psychological Health in Family Systems*. New York: Brunner/Mazel.

Lewis, Jerry M., and J. G. Looney. 1983. *The Long Struggle: Well-functioning Working-class Black Families*. New York: Brunner/Mazel.

McGill, Arthur. 1982. *Suffering: A Test of Theological Method*. Philadelphia: Westminster Press.

Murphy, Albert T. 1981. *Special Children, Special Parents: Personal Issues with Handicapped Children*. Englewood Cliffs, N.J.: Prentice-Hall.

Murphy, Judith K. 1986. *Sharing Care: The Christian Ministry of Respite Care*. New York: United Church Press.

Parker, Susan. 1980. "Parents with Mentally Retarded Down's Syndrome Children: Their Experiences with the Child and the Impact of a Short-term Educationally Oriented Group on Their Adjustment." Doctoral dissertation, University of Tennessee.

Perske, Robert. 1981. *Hope for the Families*. Nashville: Abingdon Press.

Preheim-Bartel, Dean A., and Aldred H. Neufeldt. 1986. *Supportive Care in the Congregation*. Akron, Pa.: Mennonite Central Committee.

Stinnett, N. 1984. *Relationships in Marriage and the Family*. New York: Macmillan Co.

_____ and J. DeFrain. 1985. *Secrets of Strong Families*. Boston: Little, Brown & Co.

U.S. Bureau of the Census. 1987. *Statistical Abstract of the United States: 1988* (108th ed.). Washington, D.C.: U.S. Government Printing Office.

Wilke, Harold H. 1980. *Creating the Caring Congregation: Guidelines for Ministering with the Handicapped*. Nashville: Abingdon Press.

9

Diversities of Family Membership

The common theme of this chapter is family membership. Who may one admit into one's family as a marriage partner, adult participant, or child of the family? What issues and dynamics occur if one chooses a marriage partner from outside the familiar circle? If one chooses children who are not birth children and offers to care for them permanently or temporarily, what continuities and discontinuities will one's family have with other families? It is to such questions that we now turn.

Intermarriage—Interethnic, Intercultural, Interracial

The couple electing a marriage that crosses lines of race, culture, nationality, or ethnicity will have two major sets of issues. First are the inner issues—how does a couple build a strong and healthy marriage? Second are the outer issues—how do families, neighborhoods, communities, institutions, employers, and others with whom they interact respond? We will look at these two sets of issues in turn.

Inner Issues: Building a Relationship

Both members of the marrying couple may need to examine their motives for choosing this person as mate. There has been a good bit written about motives for such marriages. These perspectives can inform the couple in its decisions.

For the most part, this research does not reveal much that is unusual in the motives for these marriages. The motive might be simply that two people come to like and eventually to love each other. They choose to marry, with little attention to race or ethnicity. Their most basic motive is the appeal of the person chosen to marry. When Ernest Porterfield carried on a study of black-white interracial marriages (by far the most emotion-laden of all the intermarriages in America) in four cities North and South, this is what he discovered: Of the forty couples he interviewed, seventy-one of the eighty individuals mentioned love and compatibility as the reasons for their marriage. There was extremely slight mention of race-related motives, or of motives arising from either partner's marginality in his or her own racial group (Porterfield 1978, pp. 62–84).

Occasionally, persons in intermarriages reveal motives that have little chance of sustaining a marriage. For example, there may be marriage as a social statement, or out of pity for the plight of a certain group. Marriage may be an act of defiance or domination. Some marry because of idealized (and often false) stereotypes.

As in any marriage, a couple is wise to be as clear as it can about motives for marriage. Authentic motives based on realistic understandings of oneself and the other are an effective foundation for a good marriage. The clergy who assist the couple in preparing for marriage will serve them well by helping them achieve this clarity about motivation.

Once married, the intercultural couple may discover a number of complications to work through in building a good relationship. There may be problems in communication, for example.

The most difficult communication occurs on a nonverbal level. For Americans, nonverbal communication is mostly unconscious. For persons of some cultures (Asian, for example) nonverbal communication is quite conscious and intentional. Alice Shae, a missionary who has lived in many cultures and a partner in a Burmese-American marriage, notes (1988, pp. 2–3):

> Asians are extremely conscious of a *million* different kinds of non-verbal communication patterns, each with their separate meanings—and frequently with different meanings for different groups (for example, rubbing one's stomach may mean that you are hungry in one culture, but that you are anxious and uneasy in another one). The use of one's eyes, the positioning of parts of the body (such as hands or feet), the way one opens or closes a door, the way one uses a stirring spoon while cooking (for example, banging it on the pot if a person is angry with one's mate), and many, many more speak much more strongly than any words a person can say.
>
> In some cultures, the strongest form of non-verbal communication is silence. It may speak of strong anger, of strong disagreement, of mistrust, etc., and one must learn to read the meaning of the silences also.
>
> Another aspect is in some cultures people speak openly and freely with one another, and often their words are taken lightly and soon forgotten. In

other cultures, people are very careful of what they say so when they speak, it has deep meaning and is taken seriously.

There is also nonverbal communication through facial expression, gesture, dress, vocal inflection, kind and degree of physical contact.

Then there is verbal communication. Richard Markoff identifies some challenges to communication between marital partners of various cultures. The first example is, what does one mean when one says "yes"? In some cultures (mostly Eastern) people say "no" only in extreme situations, so their "yes" may be qualified and filled with questions. They may desire to please or not to offend, and so say "yes." In some cultures (mostly Western) people say "no" quite freely, so a "yes" may mean enthusiastic affirmation. Saying "Thank you" is a second area of potential confusion. In Japanese culture, such expressions are offered only in situations calling for some degree of formality. An American wife might feel hurt because her Japanese husband did not thank her for a birthday gift. A Japanese wife might be confused by her American husband's "Thank you," and wonder why she was being treated like a stranger! Colloquialisms also present problems. They are constantly changing and vary from culture to culture, including those which have a fair amount of language in common (Markoff, in Tseng 1977, pp. 51–54). For example, how would these colloquialisms sound in another language or culture: "He's a chip off the old block. . . . I'm tickled to death. . . . Get your rear end in gear"?

McGoldrick and Preto have noted four areas where communication problems are likely to occur in ethnically intermarried couples: "(1) Style of communication: verbal, taciturn, rational, dramatically expressive, etc.; (2) handling of conflict: argument, reasoning, withdrawal, teasing, indirect response; (3) attitude toward intimacy and dependence: positive, fearful, assertive, demanding, withholding; and (4) attitude toward grief and sadness: stoic, expressive, emotional, denying, angry" (1984, p. 355).

There may be yet another communication issue. Some international couples marry with little or no knowledge of each other's language. One husband, a partner in an international marriage where each had a developing but still elementary knowledge of the other's language, spoke of this: "Sometimes a complex problem comes up. We know we don't have enough knowledge of either language to talk it out and settle it. That's frustrating. The positive side to this is that we don't spend time hassling in minor issues as many couples we observe seem to do!"

Each intercultural couple will have to determine what pattern or patterns will be used in family communication. Then each partner will have to learn the meaning of both the nonverbal and the verbal communication used by the spouse.

Another area which the intermarried couple will need to explore is that of values. This becomes complicated, because most persons tend to feel that their culturally ordained values are right, true, or the best. They may have become so much a part of a person that they are unconscious and unobtrusive—until one is confronted with a contrasting value.

While there is variation within each culture, there are also some basic value themes in each culture. Markoff notes,

> Despite recent trends, the acquisition of material wealth, competitive success, and upward social movement remain important values for a great many North Americans. In contrast, in Polynesian cultures, individual striving for material success often has a lower value than the maintenance of cooperative and mutually interdependent relationships within the family group and within the larger Polynesian community. In the traditional cultures of Japan and China, dignity, and the regard and esteem of others is a highly important value; while in Occidental cultures, independence in thought and action is especially valued (Markoff, in Tseng 1977, pp. 54–55).

One of those basic value questions may be on the subject of family. Is a newly married couple a new family, or part of a larger extended family? Do its resources (including earnings, savings, space in their home, food on their table) belong to them? Or are they freely available for extended family members? How wide a family circle? People from the West tend to answer that the couple is a new family entitled to its own resources. People from an Eastern country may tend to see the couple as part of a larger family and expect the couple to contribute to its welfare when needed.

Still another issue for the couple is how it will deal with its diverse ethnic-cultural roots. One observer has suggested that the options are fourfold: (1) Nonethnic intermarriage (ethnicity is not emphasized); (2) all-ethnic intermarriage (one partner fully participates in the ethnicity of the other); (3) dichotomous intermarriage (each partner goes his or her way ethnically); or (4) blended intermarriage (an attempt to gain the "best of both worlds" by sensitivity to the other, joint participation at times, pursuing one's own ethnic heritage at other times) (Murguia 1982, p. 112). Intermarriage couples need to recognize what is important to each. Then they will need to negotiate a marital lifestyle that incorporates these elements.

The process becomes even more complex with the birth of children. Every culture has its theory of child development, and these theories are markedly different one from another. Even when a couple may feel it has worked through cultural differences, the arrival of the first child is likely to bring some new conflicts over culture (Mann and Waldron, in Tseng 1977, p. 65). Birth will bring powerful emotional memories to each parent of her or his own childhood, as well as hopes for the child. Varying cultures have both different goals for the adult human and varying parental techniques to help the parent bring the child to adulthood. For example, at what age is a child weaned? The answers (from culture to culture) range from 5 months to 5 years and 7 months. At what age is a child toilet trained? The range of answers is from 4 months to 4 years and 8 months (ibid., p. 62). Should a child be constantly carried and cuddled by the mother? Should he or she be isolated, left to be aware of personal needs, to cry and assert himself or herself before needs are met? The answer varies from culture to culture. When and how is a child taught how to speak? In some cultures, this is quite informal; in others it is not. Some Polynesian cultures have an official "first word" that a child must speak. Once that word is uttered, the whole community enters into teaching the child to speak. Mann and Waldron note, "Each developmental stage [of the child] whether it involves issues of dependency, autonomy, power, skill mastery, sex identification, values, educational experiences, or peer relations, will more easily create conflicts when the culturally different parents adhere to variant prescriptions of how to achieve desired behaviors" (ibid., p. 66).

Especially in intermarriages, the ingredients that make for good marriage are needed in great supply—tolerance for diversity, a positive attitude toward change, flexibility, a sense of joy and humor, and commitment to the marriage.

Our research has made us aware that cultural differences in marriage are more widespread than we previously realized. We recall a couple who had just learned their child has a learning disability. The woman was shedding many tears. Her husband commented gently, "She's Italian—she cries. I'm Irish—I fight. At most, my eyes mist when a patriotic song is played." This man's observation offers a clue for us all. Virtually every marriage deals with some intercultural issues. These may be one European heritage to another; one section of America to another; rural-urban; laboring class–professional class, or others. Earlier in this section, we listed challenges to cross-cultural communication. This list applies to many, many couples of seemingly slight cultural difference. One of the gifts church leaders may offer all people planning and building marriages is to help the partners be clear about their own and their partner's cultural heritage regarding marriage and family. Then we can help them achieve a dialogue across their cultural differences.

The Outer Issues: Dealing with Those Beyond the Core Family

There is yet another complication. Some intermarriages operate in an inhospitable environment.

At some time in their history, thirty-three states have had laws prohibiting one or more forms of racial intermarriage (Porterfield 1978, p. 10). As late as 1966, seventeen states still had such prohibitions. The last ones of these were overturned with a United States Supreme Court ruling rendered June 12, 1967. Attitudes about intermarriage will not change as quickly as a court's ruling. And so the persons entering a mixed marriage may need to anticipate that at some points they will encounter criticism, resistance, and hampering actions.

A variety of factors may enter into just how inhospitable the outside environment is. Intermarriage is usually one of four types: (1) interracial; (2) interfaith; (3) interclass; and (4) interethnic. Studies seem to indicate that the strongest barrier to intermarriage is race, followed by religion. Then comes future social class (that is, educational level compatibility), ethnicity, and past social class. An accumulation of more than one of these differences brings about greater resistance to intermarriage (Murguia 1982, pp. 31–35). The greater the perceived differences between the two races, or religions, or ethnic groups, or classes, the greater is the social resistance as well.

There are also geographical differences in the strength of these factors. In some parts of the country, there might be very low acceptance. On the other hand, in other parts (Hawaii, for example) intermarriage is scarcely noticed. In traveling from one place to another, or through a lifetime, the intercultural couple may well experience quite varied attitudes about their intermarriage. One interracial couple, who married in the 1960s, reported a much more accepting attitude now toward their and other intermarriages than they experienced in an earlier era.

Whatever the climate, the couple will need to deal with it. Some couples have carried on a courtship in virtual secrecy. It is impossible to maintain secrecy in a marriage.

Probably the first of the groups the couple will engage will be their own families of origin. The next will likely be their extended families. If enough family support or at least acceptance can be gained so that a wedding can be arranged that affirms each family's background, an important first step to possible marital success has been taken. This might well mean two weddings, one in the style of each ethnic group, nationality, or religion from which the marriage partners come, or it might mean a wedding and celebration that integrates customs important to each. This is a place where ministers can be both sensitive and creative, and thus help the couple and their families build a beginning base of support. The worst possible scenario is that either or both families are so unaccepting that the couple is denied contact or continued membership in that family.

Another group the couple will need to engage may be the religious institutions. Does the couple seek a church-blessed marriage? Do they desire participation from clergy of both partners' backgrounds? Will this be granted? Once that issue is resolved, there is the further question of acceptance in the church community. In his study of black-white marriages, Porterfield noted a very small percentage of the forty couples he interviewed were involved in church life. A number of them had left their religious group after marrying (Porterfield 1978, pp. 51, 137–139).

Another area to be engaged is the community where the couple lives. Do they feel free to socialize, to attend public functions, to eat in restaurants? Do they find adequate dental, medical, hospital care? Do they experience cooperation and acceptance with schools, police, other community agencies?

Another outside consideration has to do with finance and housing. Are they given access to all the housing that might be available to persons in their income range? Is it unusually hard to gain credit in order to purchase housing or other needed articles? Does the couple need a larger than usual down payment? A wife in an international couple told us, "We experienced some difficulties in gaining housing, not because we were of a mixed marriage, but because my husband is Asian. We both shared in the experience of Asians seeking housing in this community."

The preceding list mentions many of the outside issues that intermarrying couples encounter on occasion in some places. One hopes that in time these issues will recede so that those who undertake these marriages may do so in a more supportive environment.

Adopting Families

Other families face a quite different issue in regard to family membership. They want to admit children into the family who were not born into it. And they have every intention of giving to these children full family rights, including those of inheritance. This family style has existed since time immemorial, but it too is undergoing great changes today.

Perhaps we can best introduce the current situation in adoption by identifying and debunking several myths about adoption. Some of them were never true. Some once were but are not anymore.

Myth one: Adoption is a second-class process. The fact is that adoption is an important process, by which persons who desire children and children who need families are brought together. In some cultures, it has been highly honored. It has not been well treated in our society, however.

Myth two: Adoption is freely available and inexpensive to any who want to undertake it. Many persons have such a "yesterday" understanding of adoption. In previous days, there may indeed have been more available children than parents. That is no longer true. Now adoptive parents wait years, endure difficulties, and spend thousands of dollars out of determination to adopt a child.

Increasing numbers of young mothers either elect legal abortion or choose to keep their babies. Currently, fewer than five in one hundred young women with an unplanned pregnancy make adoption plans. This contributes to a shortage of babies. Forty white couples will wait three to six years for each infant that is available! (Johnston 1984, p. 37).

The children who can be adopted will more likely be older children, handicapped children, sibling groups, or international children. When hopeful parents make the adjustment to the situation, they may well find such a child to adopt. Still, the process will be slow and difficult.

Persons must be prepared to spend considerable amounts of money, in addition to their time and frustration. It costs anywhere from a few hundred to many thousands of dollars to complete an adoption. Among the costs are health care of mother and child and delivery costs; transportation of the child (perhaps from another part of the country or world); agency expenses; and legal fees. A family with excellent health insurance will almost certainly experience an injustice. They will discover this insurance does not cover the hospital and delivery costs of a child they adopt when it would cover all those costs had they birthed a child!

We do know an adoption story that is something of an exception to the typical experience of delay and frustration. A friend told us how he and his wife decided to adopt "the most needy child on the agency list." When they told an adoption agency of their decision, they were shown "a wall full of pictures" and asked what they "would not accept." Refusing to choose or list exceptions, they repeated their request for the "most needy child on your list." Finally convinced of their seriousness, after only six days the worker introduced them to a 2-year-old boy. Needless to say, the child had experienced much rejection and pain. It took time for faithful parenting to overcome his fears. But our friend affirms the worth of it all.

Myth three: Adopting families should beware, because the adopted child may contain "bad blood" or may be of "bad stock." Actually every person is a combination of inherited characteristics and learned behavior. Nobody has successfully isolated the roles of these factors, so such a statement about the dominance of heredity is untrue. There is another related, unfortunate myth.

Myth four: Adopted children get into more trouble than children who live in the families into which they were born. Persons have been known to perpetuate that myth without careful study to see if it is true. Information to date indicates that it is not.

What, then, is the process by which persons become adoptive parents? For many, this process begins with the discovery of infertility. Some, such as a single person who wants to be a parent, may desire adoption for other reasons.

At some point the couple or the individual decides to attempt adoption. Edmund Blair Bolles advises those starting the search to be in touch with two types of organizations. One is the adoptive parent associations. While not placement agencies, these are groups banded together because of mutual concerns. Some associations are advocates on behalf of adoptive or would-be adoptive parents. Others are advocates on behalf of the older child needing adoption. These groups are helpful for information, counseling, and encouragement (see Bolles 1984, pp. 223–248 for a listing of known parent associations).

The would-be adopters will also need to locate, select, and enter into a process with those who help bring about adoptions. There are a number of choices available. (The associations just mentioned can often help folks locate more agencies than one can find in the phone book and give some experience and perspective on each.)

There are both public and private agencies. Many of them may well have such lengthy waiting lists that they will be rather discouraging. This is quite likely for couples wanting infants.

Some, sensing the length of the wait or for other reasons, may elect some other directions for their adoption. They may pursue an international adoption. Most of these children come from Korea, the Philippines, Hong Kong, India, and some countries of Latin America.

Some seek an independent adoption. In this, the couple uses attorneys but not an agency to locate a child, negotiate the adoption, and complete it. A potential adoptable child is discovered in a variety of ways. For example, advertisements may be placed in newspapers. Persons who answer are screened until a suitable fit is achieved. This is legal in most states, but it can veer into illegality all too easily. The issue seems, in the main, to be that it is legal and reasonable to pay the mother surrendering a child for legal, medical, and perhaps living expenses. However, it is not legal to "buy" a child. One social worker commented, "While persons may gain an adopted child more quickly in this manner, I would use caution. Some of the things an adoption agency does may seem cumbersome, but these steps may assure readiness for adoption and a good fit. Families may be helped to accept the reality of their situation, do grief about it, and be ready for an adoptive child. If persons pursue this course, I urge them to seek counseling about their family development as well."

Each of these methods—agency or independent adoption, seeking infant, older child, or international child—has its advantages and disadvantages. These would include length of waiting time, cost, and risk. Fortunate are those who have found that support group of people who have undergone the same challenges. Those who describe the process call it the "adoption maze."

Whatever the means chosen, there will be delays, a home evaluation (that may include visits with both spouses together and individually), more waiting, and perhaps eventually the placement of a child. Veterans of this process advise phone calls every few months, followed by letters to the adoption agency confirming what was said. They urge potential parents to be present at any and all information meetings and to make themselves known to those leading the meetings. And they advise that long waits—often years—are part of the process. There are no guarantees that the long waits will be rewarded. Couples are wise to keep all their options open in seeking that child to love and welcome into their family.

There are at least two very lively issues in adoption. One of these is whether assumptions and practices around adoption should be changed. Jeanne Warren Lindsay writes to advocate "open adoption," a process that allows the birth mother to be more involved. As one who has worked with pregnant teenagers, she rejoices to find this option. Up until recently, she notes, the pregnant teenage young woman seemingly had only two choices—keeping the child (and she might not be ready to be a parent) or abortion. The third option, adoption, was seldom chosen. Somehow carrying a child to full term and then being shut off from it forever, with no contact or information, seemed to be more pain than they could bear. By contrast, in open adoption the birth parent(s) will have choices. They may choose the adoptive parents from descriptions and pictures. (Of course, this list has been screened by the agency.) They may talk with one or more potential adoptive sets of parents on the phone or, in some instances, meet them face to face. There may be some ongoing contact, by phone or correspondence. Lindsay sees this as a means by which some unmarried mothers are able to give up children to caring adoptive families. These young mothers would not have done so under other conditions. They were able to do so with more dignity, and at least a little less pain, than in other ways (Lindsay 1987, pp. 14–28).

The other controversial issue is whether cross-racial adoptions are ever in the child's best interest. There are groups of professionals who say no. Others, including those carrying out cross-racial adoptions, experience real gain and enrichment for persons of both races in such a family life. This is particularly so if parents are careful to educate the child about the child's ethnic roots and provide participation in groups with these ethnic roots as well as those of the family in which the child is raised. Those who work with adoptive families need to be aware that these controversies are going on, and in turn influence the families on the advisability, and even the possibility, of some types of adoption.

Through some of the processes described above, finally the child is welcomed into the home. What then? Successful adoptive parenting, in the view of Jerome Smith and Franklin Miroff (in Johnston 1984), depends on the family's successfully completing a process of building a sense of *entitlement*. This is a true sense of belonging, the child to the parent, the parent to the child. It is a recognition that family is a spiritual reality made possible by relationships rather than "blood" ties. Building entitlement is an ongoing process of growth, rather than a single task. There are at least three subtasks that contribute to entitlement.

The first is "learning to recognize and deal with the psychological ramifications of their own infertility" or other reasons preventing a birth child (cited in Johnston 1984, p. 17). This involves coming to grips with the reality that long-held assumptions may not prove to be true. Then there will be the task of dealing with the feelings, whatever they may be, that come from that realization. This will be a grief experience, and likely grief feelings—denial, anger, bargaining, depression, and acceptance—may be part of it.

The second subtask is "coming to recognize that adoptive parenting is different from biological parenting in a number of significant and unavoidable ways" (ibid.). One way to understand some of this change is as *role handicap*. When persons assume a role without assuming with it all of the role's expectations, there is role handicap. The roles of both parent and child in adoptive families have this aspect. They attempt to be parent and child to each other, but have become that in ways different from the majority of society. They can deal with this either by acknowledging the differences or by denying and ignoring them entirely. The latter course was seen in adoptions of a generation or two ago, when parents tried to hide the facts of adoption. When this course did not prove advisable, then folks attempted to act as though the difference did not matter.

However, adoption is different in a number of ways. Laws on adoption point to some of the differences. Adoptees (and they only) are denied access to their own birth records. Exceptions are granted occasionally by the courts but usually not until the child attains his or her majority. While the adoptee is included in adoptive parents' inheritance, she or he is not included in adoptive grandparents' inheritance, unless specifically mentioned. In some states, incest and intermarriage laws do not apply to adoptees (Johnston 1984, p. 30).

Frequently, adoptive children do not look like their parents. This is particularly true in a cross-racial or cross-ethnic adoption, but it is true for many others as well. This may create questions both within and without the family.

Every adoptive family lives with two hard issues: belonging and identity. Belonging issues exist for both parent and child. Adoptive parents tell of nightmares in which someone comes to claim their child—and these nightmares occur both before and after the court hearing that gives them full legal custody.

Adopted children have their issue of belonging also. One adoptive father told us, "I think there is a burden each adopted child carries. At birth, a parent decided not to keep that child." Some adopted children ask why the birth mother chose to do this. Many adoptive parents confess this is a most difficult question to answer. For one thing, they are not privy to that person's motives. For another, many of the suggested answers, such as "You are a chosen child," seemed inaccurate and dishonest. Parents may be reduced to assuming, and telling the child, that the birth parent did it out of sacrificial love for the child. They can go on to say how happy they are that the birth parent made it possible for this child to come to this home! Not all adopted children are concerned. For those who are, that answer will probably not satisfy them.

There is the related issue—identity. Starting with the decision by a parent not to keep the child, and continuing with a total lack of information about and contact with one's birth family, an adopted child has handicaps in knowing his or her identity. For some, not all, this is indeed a formidable handicap. A woman in her thirties, an adopted child herself and parent of an adopted child, told us, "Every year on my birthday, I wonder about my birth mother, and I'll bet she wonders about me. I'd like to talk to her just once. I'd tell her I'm doing OK and that I adopted a child myself. I'd like to see if I look like her. I went to the home for unwed mothers where I was born and tried to trace her. Although I was unsuccessful, the director remembered my mother. She told me her mannerisms were much like mine and that she had green eyes, like mine. That's all I have, but it means a lot to me! This has nothing to do with my love for the parents who adopted and raised me. This is an entirely different issue!"

The task, then, for adoptive families is to see their relationship as different from, but not inferior to, families built on biological relationships.

As they achieve a sense of family, they discover that love and a shared history build families. As Bolles puts it, "Families are subjective institutions, living in the mind" (Bolles 1984, p. 214).

The third subtask is "learning to handle the questions and comments of outsiders or extended family members which often will reflect society's general feeling that adoption is a second best alternative for all involved" (Johnston 1984, p. 17). Adopting families may need to help people learn terms such as "birth parent" and "adoptive parent," instead of "real parent." They may need to help people overcome negative assessments of those who would "give up" a child to which they had given birth. The adoptive family at times has to build its life and make its way in a society that does not entirely understand.

With regard to adoptive families, the bad news is that they are often a second choice, are difficult to start, and must maintain themselves in a world not totally supportive. The good news is that those hindrances do not keep many adoptive families from being extremely effective. These families have grown beautifully strong together.

Foster Families

Foster families are similar to adoptive families in that they welcome children who are not their biological children. They differ in that the welcome is for a temporary period. Furthermore, foster families are licensed in their given area and are modestly compensated for the expenses of the children in their care.

Foster families perform an important service. Circumstances may arise in some families that necessitate the children's being removed from their home, either temporarily or permanently. There might be illness or surgery, mental illness, alcoholism, or death of a parent. The children may have been abused. Parents may have fought, or been unable to provide discipline. The children may have behavior problems.

There are several different types of foster care. One of these is emergency care. A sudden problem arises in a family, and a child is placed in a foster home for no more than thirty days. Another type is "limited." In this circumstance, the arrangement is to be of temporary but uncertain duration. It is assumed the child will return to the biological family once that family's problems are resolved or improved. Still another type of placement is "preadoptive." Here it is assumed that the child will be adopted as soon as the biological parents' rights have been terminated. Another type is "permanent." It is anticipated that the child will never return home, but circumstances prevent authorities from considering adoption. This child will be in a foster home until she or he achieves majority. Then there is "specialized" foster home placement. This might include disabled children, those seriously ill, unmarried teenagers with families of their own, and others. The circumstances of these children may change their status during a stay in a foster home (Bolles 1984, p. 178).

There are foster families that designate they will care for infants, or preschool children, or elementary-school-age children, or teenagers.

Qualifying as foster parents is similar to qualifying to be adoptive parents. Adults apply to the licensing agency, experience a home study, and perhaps undergo some brief training. Then they are informed when children need foster care, and they can decide whether or not to render it.

Once a family has agreed to accept a foster child and the child has arrived, this family has a number of unique issues with which to deal. For one, they need to gain perspective on their desired attachment to or separateness from the child, then work to achieve that. They know that the child is in need of care and love. At the same time, they realize that the child may be removed from their home at any time, sometimes expectedly, sometimes not. We visited with one family who expected their foster child to remain in their home for several years. Then rather suddenly the biological parent wanted him back and "made a deal" with the court. A caseworker came to the foster home on Wednesday and told them to pack the child's belongings for a Friday departure! They appealed and succeeded in keeping him in the home until the end of the school year. They noted, however, that things changed from that moment on. Instead of building character and habits, they were all preparing themselves for separating.

A social worker with foster families notes that this issue of attachment and separation differs depending on the age of the child. With a young child, foster parents may attach quickly and have great difficulty separating. With an older child, the difficulty may be in attaching, rather than in separating. Still, for each, establishing trust and care in a setting known as temporary is an important but difficult task.

Yet another issue is the discovery of what a foster family can do and what it cannot do for a child. A foster father recalls the first foster child he and his wife welcomed. "I was entirely unrealistic," he remembers. "I thought that we could take this eleven-year-old boy, help him escape all the chaos of his life, teach him good habits, and help him grow up to be a solid Christian man. In time I discovered how powerful was the influence of the family that raised him to that point. The changes we could bring to his life were slow and difficult in coming." Allowing a child to deal with memories, feelings, and contacts with the child's family of origin is part of the foster parenting task. At the same time, there is an aspect that foster parents may not realize at the outset— serving as role models for the family of origin. The vast majority of children do return to those homes. Not only a sheltered child, but a changed family process is a worthy goal, and the foster family may contribute to that end.

Still another part of the foster family's task is to live with struggle and ambiguity. If parents come only with love and goodwill and lack appreciation for the necessity of struggle, they will quickly become disillusioned. Foster parents will need to recognize that problems are often deep-seated and require much persistence. Further, they may not know until years later—and maybe never—whether the lessons and relationships had an impact. Effective foster parents are a very special group of people!

After telling the story of their care for a preadoptive child, Evie, foster parent Lee Carlson writes, "Loving foster care is demanding, inconvenient, draining, irritating and requires sacrifice. But it is worth it, because good foster care builds healthier families . . . and there are a thousand Evies out there, waiting" (Carlson 1986, p. 2).

The Intentional Family

We will briefly mention just two other family types with membership issues. One is the "intentional family." By this we mean any group of adults, and possibly children, that may choose to form something akin to a family grouping. These adults may have kinship ties or they may not. Usually this involves acquiring a mutual residence. For example, a few adults may pool their resources so that they can afford to rent or buy more spacious housing. Two or more single parents may share quarters so that they can exchange services with each other for food preparation and care for the children. Some intentional families are built around religious or other commitments. A group of middle-aged couples became convinced that the usual one couple, one house pattern was ecologically wasteful. And so they attempted, for a time, to live together in one large dwelling, with fewer autos serving their joint needs. Some quite intentionally attempt to build a group concept, with a total group life and ritual within the household.

These households may be rather flexible as to additions of people to the makeup of the family unit, or they may be rather firm, enduring for years without addition or subtraction. Such intentional family units have the capability of answering family needs for persons who might have no other access to family in a given location.

A Family of One

There is one other family type that should be considered. This was impressed on me (Dick) in a conversation with a colleague I admire very much. She is a professor of health sciences in a state university.

Whenever we can, we visit about the projects that are engaging us. Some time ago, I described this book project to her. She asked what were the "changing families" we were going to describe. I listed them, and she asked, "Are you going to include single persons?" (She was a mid-life, never-married single person.) I was stumped. We included single parents, and we included couples without children. But we did not mention single persons without children. Yet, when a church considers the number of "family units" or "household units" or "giving units" single persons are among them! If the church were to be divided up into clusters of families, either geographically or by the ages of the adults, my friend the single adult would want to be included. At times, her church had been important extended family to her. Her home was a place of hospitality where groups could gather. She took interest in, and contributed to, the religious education of children and youth in her church, particularly when she could use her expertise as a health educator. After our conversation, I was still stumped. Is a single person a family? What services that churches render to families should they be equally careful to render to singles?

The diversity of families in our changing world is truly amazing. There seems to be a family drive so strong that family-type bonds can be formed in many different ways.

The Response of Faith and Faith Community

The issues of the families described in this chapter aroused deep empathy in these writers. We found ourselves face to face with the "Christ and culture" issues. We came to long for a Christ-trans-forming-culture perspective and strategy on behalf of these families. With this in mind, let's look at each of the family types in turn.

First the intermarried families. How much more strongly "culture" speaks than does "Christ" in most of our attitudes! Up to now, we have avoided the value question that we now face: *Should* such persons intermarry? For us, the biblical-theological answer is a resounding *yes*!—if they see each other clearly, love what they see, and are willing to take on the additional effort needed to build a strong intermarriage.

To be sure, there are times when the Bible speaks of intermarriage in less than complimentary terms. Rebekah complained of Esau's foreign wives (Gen. 27:46), and much later Ezra commanded Israelites to separate from their foreign wives for the sake of returning to the covenant (Ezra 10). But these are minor themes dealing with historical particularities.

The major themes include: God as creator, who made all humankind in God's image—male and female, and all the races and nations of humankind; a God who is referred to in terms of father and mother;

a book of the Bible (Ruth) that celebrates international friendship and marriage; a Christ who expresses God's love for the world and who breaks down dividing walls and barriers between us; a new humanity where there is neither Jew nor Greek, slave nor free, male nor female. All believers in God-in-Christ are one in union with Jesus Christ.

When one applies these basic, indisputable Christian theological understandings to an intermarriage, the conclusion seems absolutely clear. God blesses these children of God in their marriage covenant and cares for their well-being. And so should the Christian church.

Within this atmosphere of affirmation, the minister doing premarital counseling with an intermarrying couple will feel free to probe, question, and challenge to help each individual be as clear as possible about who the other is, and what may be some of the complications of their commitment. If they decide to proceed, sensitive pastors will offer them dignified services of Christian marriage that reflect their diversity of heritage and all the resources that churches offer couples to build a strong marriage and a healthy family.

One of these resources may be simply to open the door of conversation so that the couple may talk about their marriage if they wish. Too frequently this is an avoided topic. Another of these resources may be frankness and openness about how the church and other communities are doing in accepting this couple. A pastor or other church leader may want to tell a couple, "We aspire to be a loving church for all people. But we are human and we are diverse. Will you let us know from time to time how we are doing?" Too often, a church that is trying to be supportive will lose such a couple when an isolated ethnic or racial slur comes that couple's way. Without discussion, the couple may feel this is the unspoken attitude of most folks at the church and withdraw.

If the Christian church can be a place where people deal with their discomforts and come to comprehend each other, that learning can have rich transferability to other communities the couple enters. And members of the majority culture in the original community may have important learnings to take elsewhere as well.

There is a risk for the local church that attempts to be this kind of community. The risk is that the presence of persons of other races and cultures (and the intermarriages) may make other members so uncomfortable they withdraw. The persons who withdraw will probably have such inner turmoil between Christian ideals and ingrained cultural prejudices that they may not even admit to themselves the reason they left.

A church may need to ask: Is our vision of a redeemed and reconciled humanity so central that we will take this risk and live with the consequences? It is our hope that at least a few churches in every community will answer yes.

The issues around adoptive, foster, and intentional families are not so emotional. Biblical mandates to care for the homeless, the widow, and the orphan are frequent and clear. Paul takes up the image of "adoption" as a beloved metaphor to describe God's acceptance of us into God's family. Adoption is one way to say salvation. Through Christ we are in God's family, and joint heirs with Christ. Bible-reading Christians ought to know, therefore, that we are all adopted children! As a matter of fact, a Bible scholar pointed out to us that most translations disguise this truth some of the time. The word that should be translated "adoption" is instead translated "sonship." Adoption is a much more central biblical teaching than we often realize. Therefore we have reason to be deeply accepting and supportive of families who offer their homes to others.

For the adoptive family this might mean moral support through the long waiting process. When the child arrives the church might offer the same or parallel type of celebration as at the arrival of a birth child—showers, meals, welcome visits, cards, letters, and gifts. If the church sends special gifts to birth families, it should send them to adoptive families as well. The church can affirm the first-class status of this adoptive family and can welcome the child as a new member of that extended family that is the Christian church. Perhaps this will take place in services of child-parent dedication, baptism, or special rituals celebrating the adoption.

We recently visited with a couple who had three birth children and then had complications that caused any further pregnancies to be inadvisable. Over the next few years they adopted two Korean daughters. Our conversation with them revealed two other points about supportive church families. For one thing, they said, "Don't make such a big deal of this. We did this as much for ourselves as for the children. We wanted a large family. Sometimes people fuss so over our Korean children that our other children wonder what's the matter with them. Nobody notices them." The other insight arose incidentally. They mentioned that they would have loved to accept a group of international siblings, but that the several-thousand-dollar cost per child prevented their doing that. Perhaps this would have been a place their church could have helped. Those who want to open their home but lack the funds for an expensive adoption process might have loving financial backing from church members, groups, or funds.

Another opportunity may occur when a young unmarried woman in church discovers she is pregnant. Caring persons can interpret to her the thought that though it would be painful to carry this pregnancy to term, deliver a child, and give it up, this would be a very special gift to some waiting family. One adoptive father called the act of giving up one's child for adoption the ultimate act of love.

There is one other area that deserves the attention of Christian leaders. Repeatedly persons described the adoption process as overly bureaucratic, outmoded, understaffed, and in general suffering from lack of attention and resources. Church groups might want to serve as advocates to improve adoption procedures on behalf of all children and families desiring adoption. Until the process improves, existing adoptive families can serve as resources and encouragers to those attempting to make adoptions.

As for foster families, virtually every community struggles to find homes that offer quality foster child care. Perhaps the church can be aware of this community need and recruit among its members persons with the gifts to respond to these children.

With regard to intentional families, church leaders might want to stop and reflect: Are there any intentional families in our church? in our community? In what ways do these groups have needs parallel to more conventional families and in what ways do they have unique family needs? How can the Christian church be responsive and helpful?

If the consciousness is raised, churches can find much to offer intentional families and singles. Perhaps churches can encourage folks who would find mutual benefit in the development of intentional family groupings. For example, a lonely older person needing attention but living in a spacious home might be teamed with a young family needing a place to live. Churches may be led to understand clearly that truly they are actually a larger intentional family (filled with adoptees), an extended family that includes all family units, including those units with one member.

Resources and References

Baptiste, David A., Jr. 1984. "Marital and Family Therapy with Racially/Culturally Intermarried Stepfamilies: Issues and Guidelines." *Family Relations*, vol. 33, pp. 373–380.

Bolles, Edmund Blair. 1984. *The Penguin Adoption Handbook*. New York: Viking Press.

Canape, Charlene. 1986. *Adoption: Parenthood Without Pregnancy*. New York: Avon Books.

Carlson, Lee. 1986. "A Beginning for Evie." *American Baptist Churches of the Central Region Newsletter*, August, p. 2.

Cerroni-Long, E. L. 1985. "Marrying Out: Socio-Cultural and Psychological Implications of Intermarriage." *Journal of Comparative Studies*, vol. 16, no. 1 (Spring), pp. 25–45.

Cretser, Gary A., and Joseph J. Leon, eds. 1982. *Intermarriage in the United States*. New York: Haworth Press.

Ertl, Carol. 1981. "Strengthening Foster Families." In Nick Stinnett, John DeFrain, et al., eds., *Family Strengths and Roots of Well Being*. Lincoln, Neb.: University of Nebraska Press.

Johnston, Patricia Irwin. 1984. *An Adoptor's Advocate*. Fort Wayne, Ind.: Perspectives Press.

Lindsay, Jeanne Warren. 1987. *Open Adoption: A Caring Option*. Buena Park, Calif.: Morning Glory Press.

Mandell, Betty Reid. 1973. *Where Are the Children?* Lexington, Mass.: D. C. Heath & Co.

Mann, Eberhard, and Jane A. Waldron. 1977. "Intercultural Marriage and Child Rearing." In Tseng Wen-Shing, John F. McDermott, Jr., and Thomas W. Maretzki, eds., *Adjustment in Intercultural Marriage*. Honolulu: University Press of Hawaii.

Markoff, Richard. 1977. "Intercultural Marriage: Problem Areas." In Tseng Wen-Shing, John F. McDermott, Jr., and Thomas W. Maretzki, eds., *Adjustment in Intercultural Marriage*. Honolulu: University Press of Hawaii.

McGoldrick, Monica, and Nydia Garcia Preto. 1984. "Ethnic Intermarriage: Implications for Therapy." *Family Process*, vol. 23 (Sept.), pp. 347–364.

Murguia, Edward. 1982. *Chicano Intermarriage: A Theoretical and Empirical Study*. San Antonio, Tex.: Trinity University Press.

Porterfield, Ernest. 1978. *Black and White Mixed Marriages*. Chicago: Nelson-Hall.

Shae, Alice. 1988. Personal correspondence (Sept. 25).

Simon, Rita. 1988. "Transracial Adoption Is in a Child's Best Interest." *American Family*, March, pp. 1–2.

Tseng Wen-Shing, John F. McDermott, Jr., and Thomas W. Maretzki, eds. 1977. *Adjustment in Intercultural Marriage*. Honolulu: University Press of Hawaii.

10

The Caring
Church's Response

We have now reflected on the evolution of the family and a theology of the changing family. Furthermore, we have explored a number of changing family styles. Out of all this, what do we conclude? What is the responsible church leader to do?

It has not been our intent to increase the guilt level of already overburdened church leaders. Yet that may be the inevitable result for caring folks who hear about more family needs.

One minister who offers creative family ministries reported feeling this crunch of responsibility. As the Rev. Dr. Bob L. Rhymer of Columbus, Ohio, wrote us:

> Since finishing my doctor of ministry to marriage and family degree at Eastern Baptist Seminary, I have been even more frustrated than before. This is true because: (1) I'm aware of more that needs to be done because of my increased knowledge; (2) the local church often has little understanding and appreciation of what we could be doing in family ministry; and (3) my job description, while it doesn't prevent me from doing family ministry, doesn't allow much time for specific family programming—that is, if I do all that is expected of me in other areas.

That's the issue. A reader could well comment, "A comprehensive ministry to families, including changing families, is a wonderful idea considered in a vacuum. But how do you fit it into an already crowded church agenda or a small church's program?" This is a question we cannot take lightly. Our response is threefold.

First of all, in this book we are calling for a shift in perspective about what family ministry *is*. We are not defining family ministry simply as more programs for families. Rather than urging congregations and pastors to create more and more family programs, we are calling instead for more family support. We see the fundamental role of congregations as sources of family support and the role of church leaders as coordinators of that support. Some illustrations from earlier chapters will help to make the point clear.

In chapter 2 we suggested the church should challenge the cultural assumption that paid work is *the* measure of a person's worth. The insights of househusbands and housewives provoked us to suggest activities such as taking a church vacation and linking couples with similar occupational concerns for mutual support. Our programmatic suggestions were largely aimed at creating support groups of folks in similar situations. We advocated attention to child care.

In chapter 3, where we confronted the great needs of single parents, the key concept of ministry we offered was support through networking. Single parents need support emotionally, for building their self-esteem and for linking with each other. Three levels of support were described: formal supports, such as professional helpers offer; structured informal supports of groups *for* single parents and groups that *include* single parents in their regular activities; informal linkages of friends and kin. Our research showed that in fact single parents seek most the informal support of friends and groups.

In chapter 4 we raised the question of how a congregation could be supportive of blended families and pointed out the need to consider the church schedule. One strategy that congregations have found to be helpful is scheduling major educational and fellowship activities of the church on a week night. This recognizes that children from blended families or single-parent homes may be visiting the other parent on weekends. In chapter 5 we identified approaches that need to be incorporated into the practice of clergy so that they can minister with families who have religious and value differences. We have contended that the *way* church activities are promoted and carried out is often more important in ministry with changing families than adding a special program for a particular family type.

In chapter 6 we suggested that congregations consider how hospitable they are to couples who for whatever reason do not come with children attached. And in chapter 7 we again asked churches to consider how their schedule and climate of acceptance can be adapted to the needs of families living with space and time issues.

Chapter 8 made the concept of family support central to ministry with families whose members have disabilities. We focused on the need such families have for inclusion in the normal life of the church and outlined several ways congregations could offer these households concrete assistance, such as respite care and even lifelong support groups.

Finally, in chapter 9, we considered how pastors and churches can offer support to an even wider diversity of family groups. We explored the concerns of those involved in intercultural marriage, adoption, and foster care. We included intentional families and single persons in order to sharpen the focus on support as the critical ingredient in family ministries.

In short, we call for a paradigm shift away from a singleminded programmatic focus toward a focus on family support. To provide family support calls upon the congregation and its leaders to reconsider such issues as the climate of receptiveness, interpretation of program, and schedule at least as often as it calls for the addition of programs to the agenda.

Second, in this book we call for the inclusion of changing families in the regular programs and life of the congregation. In fact, we are convinced that most churches are doing more for changing families than they realize. For example, they are providing a supportive base for the ones already in their midst. And since there is continuity from "traditional families" to "changing" families, activities offered may serve both. Parenting groups can be helpful both to married and to single parents. Couples communication groups can be effective for couples with children, couples without children, interethnic-racial-national couples, two-career couples, and commuter couples (when they can be there).

Third, we believe that some modest changes can make this ministry with changing families through existing programs more effective. Some of these changes may be "only" in wording, atmosphere, and attitude. Responding to single parents with expressions of confidence in their strengths and warmth for them as persons were two suggestions in chapter 3 that illustrate such changes. Scheduling important congregational events so that children of blended families can participate is another modest change suggested in chapter 4. In chapter 5 the thrust of our message to churches with families with religious value conflicts is that congregations address through their adult education activities the issues raised by these families. Mourning with childless couples the death of a dream, as described in chapter 6, calls for adapting and applying the ordinary ministry of grieving in community to this special situation. And surely celebrating when families with space and time issues *can* participate in the life of the congregation, as advocated in chapter 7, illustrates a simple change in attitude that makes all the difference for such families.

Church leaders need to keep in mind that they are not called to do everything. Rather, their call is to discern the gifts of their congregation's members and discover how those particular persons can respond to the unique challenges that belong to their situation.

There are steps churches can take to discover which family groups in their midst most need their care. Ways can then be discovered to make appropriate responses, either through the efforts of one congregation or through a family of churches. How is this done? We suggest that fitting discoveries occur when congregations undertake four delicately interrelated tasks. These four tasks are: a strategic task, a theological task, an educational task, and an advocacy task. We shall consider each one in turn.

A Strategic Task

The individuals or groups of people who are convinced the church should be more helpful to changing families have at least a threefold strategic task.

First, they need to develop a strategy for family ministry in their church. They will need to ask many questions as to how changed attitudes and possible new ministries will be implemented in their church. Is there an existing board that has this responsibility already, or does it need to be assigned? Is there a long-range planning committee that might be open to input about ministry with the changing family? Does a new board or task force need to be created? Or does an ad hoc approach work best in their congregation?

Bob Rhymer discovered that the church he served did not wish to create a separate family life committee. Their style was to work within the existing church structure. So family life was included as one of the program focuses of the church. When church goals were written, family life goals were included.

A second aspect of the strategic task has to do with identifying needs among families in both the church and the community. If we are going to respond, to what family type should or can we respond? What is needed and wanted among those we care for in our community?

There are several ways to get this information. One is to interview various types of families in the church. Through interviews you will discover if these folks have other friends of the same family type in the community and what they are feeling, thinking, wanting, needing for support. Since families sometimes leave the church when they have had a domestic crisis, you might want to do similar interviews with persons who have left the church in the previous year.

Another way to get relevant information is to contact organizations and agencies serving certain family types. Groups for single parents and for remarried families may be the most common. Ask them if there is need for a bridge to the faith community or if there are needs that are not being met.

Again, one might look for gaps in existing services. Is it true in your community that one in four families is a single-parent family? Quite possibly a visit with schoolteachers or principals will tell you. Do services and support groups exist for that large a population of that family type? Statistics from one's census tract will reveal information about families that could be served.

Once needs are identified, a third aspect of strategizing is: Who can best minister to these needs? Most congregations will have limited funds and resources. Who else can help? Suppose your small strategizing group decided there was a need for a series of community gatherings to explore some of the changing family types we have mentioned. You could ask your church to sponsor it. Another possibility would be to ask a group of churches, either of one denomination or of many, to undertake it. Or you might turn to a library, a school district, or a local college, university, or theological school to offer such a forum. Your group could promise to help with publicity and logistics. As planners, always ask, "Is it more important that we do it or that we see to it that it is done?"

A Theological Task

At the same time, church leaders involved in planning have a theological task. Since we have been attempting to provide theological resources throughout this book, we need not belabor this point. We simply pause to underline how absolutely important family life is for a person's most basic needs, and thus for one's theological outlook. Jesus' well-documented love for children and concern for their spiritual welfare clearly implies concern for the families into which children are born and grow to adulthood.

Our beliefs about God, sin and forgiveness, salvation and grace, and how to grow in Christian living are rooted in our family relationships. The experiences we have as we grow up in a family shape our basic beliefs. The life partnerships we form with adults further shape both our conscious and our unconscious theologies. Our theologies in turn influence our decisions about sexuality, marriage and parenthood, vocation, and life goals. Persons in healthy, strong families are likely to have healthy, strong theologies!

We have been discovering that there can be wholesome families in a variety of forms. Persons with potential for wholesome theological perspective can come out of many styles of families. Likewise, persons in a number of family types can be subject to such stress or pain that they find it very difficult to believe in a providential and gracious God of love. Providing intervention and family support so that basic personal needs are met is not only a compassionate human task, it is a theological mandate!

As we outlined in chapter 1, the Bible offers resources for affirming a variety of family configurations, including some that might be part of God's continuing creative activity. In the Bible the family is never allowed to be an end in itself. It is expected that the family will be a servant of God's redemptive intent for humankind. Therefore the Bible mandates the empowering of all families so that they can provide for the basic human needs of their members and equip them to be agents of God's redemptive power.

If we have interpreted the Bible correctly, it not only undergirds a wide diversity of families but also charges families with tremendous responsibilities. This theological understanding guides everything else we say. The church is to hold high the transforming resources of the gospel and the responsibility of all kinds of families to call forth the growing faith and witness of their members. Effective planning for ministry with changing families needs to be permeated with such a theological perspective.

An Educational Task

Planners also have an educational task, one that is double-edged: The church needs to be educated about changing families; families need to be educated about their responsibilities and opportunities.

Family advocates may want to provide an opportunity for church members to reflect on the nature of changing families. This book itself is a useful study tool. It could be used with an adult Sunday church school class or a specially gathered evening group or weekend retreat. A leader might invite resource persons who live in various family lifestyles to facilitate the discussion of each chapter. Another choice might be to invite family therapists, representatives from family advocacy groups, family life educators, or family sociologists. With the exception of the first chapter, the outline of a group discussion about each chapter would be rather similar. A discussion outline might include these questions:

1. What issues and opportunities does this type of family have in common with other families?
2. What issues and opportunities does this type of family have that are unique?
3. What is offered in our community for this type of family?
4. How can our church be more sensitive, responsive, and helpful to persons in this type of family?

5. How can we encourage and empower this type of family to fulfill its theological mandate for families? How may its patterns of behavior help family members fulfill God's intent for family?

A less demanding option would be a panel discussion of persons from varying family styles presenting a few of their experiences at a church dinner. At least the door of further discovery could be opened. Anyone with further interest could be invited to speak with the members of your group of advocates. Copies of this book could also be made available. If the planners of ministry with families have interviewed folks living in a variety of households, the sharing of their findings with the congregation will certainly help to educate the church congregation and raise its consciousness.

The second part of this task is education by the church. Much of a church's educational task here can be done with all kinds of families at once. However, those planning the educational program need to develop awareness of all the families with whom they deal. For example, a cradle-roll superintendent may need to be effective with single-parent families. A Sunday church school teacher may need to become aware of different names within the household of a stepfamily. A family life teacher may need to learn not to lay guilt trips on two-career families that have elected to put children in day-care centers. The couples class teacher may need to be sensitive to the involuntarily and voluntarily childless couples in that group. Dealing with this diversity calls for great sensitivity not only in conducting programs in the church but in publicizing and interpreting them as well. The Rev. Rick Harrison of Newark, Ohio, notes this when he writes:

> We have been careful in all of our publicity to use words that do not exclude persons who would not ordinarily consider themselves to be part of a family. We have discovered that often couples who are not married and have been dating for a long time or who are in fact living together without marriage often do not respond to programs which are designated for families. Also, we have discovered many elderly people who live alone . . . often exclude themselves because they do not consider themselves to be a part of a family.
>
> Therefore, in all of our programming we insist on groupings that mix families together. For example, if we plan intergenerational experiences we put parents and their children in different groups to avoid making those persons who are in attendance by themselves feel excluded. Also I teach a . . . class which includes both married and unmarried couples and some single persons. We are always careful in that class to avoid dealing with any issues from a couple perspective. Couples are frequently divided so that their interaction is based on their experiences as individual persons. We have discovered that this excludes no one, and couples soon begin to accept this manner of operation.

In this way, much of a church's educational program can be offered to all or most families at the same time. Family ministry education might include two broad areas, content and skills.

Content

In each content area, church leaders will help build concepts, provide information, and deepen understanding of self and others. At least four content areas should be addressed. One is the topic of growth in faith throughout a lifetime; a part of this content area is the subject of moral growth. A second content area is sexuality—helping persons accept their sexuality as a gift of God, gain comfort with it, and learn to make responsible ethical decisions about it. A third content area has to do with family relationships—Christian discipline, how relationships change as family members grow older, conflict management, forgiveness, and reconciliation. A fourth content area is recognition of the stages of life and the difficult transitions or common crises that may occur in each. Knowledge of how to cope and how to support one another in coping with such transitions is a part of this area.

Skills

Three skills areas are also a part of family education. The first is communication skills. This includes clarification skills, active listening, self-disclosure of feelings, thoughts, and beliefs, managing conflict effectively, and building esteem in oneself and others. A second skill area focuses on planning skills. Individual family members and families together need to learn how to plan for spending (and giving) money and time, for leisure activities, for education and careers, and for the care of aging family members. Intentional living in the light of the gospel requires skills that can be learned. The third area is that of organizational skills. Families will want to learn how to organize their lives so there is justice in the use of time, resources, and leisure. Families may want to know how they can organize to deal with other institutions—schools, churches, and other agencies (Leonard 1982, pp. 17–24).

Of course there are still more skills that families need to learn. One may be the ability to live with diversity within and among families. Carole Della Pia–Terry has frequently done workshops with the children of single-parent families or remarried families. She reports the lively participation and sense of relief when finally *their* family type is acknowledged and they can discuss their feelings about what is happening in their families. Quite possibly adults, young people, and children might benefit from joint discussions of the structure and dynamics of their type of family. Together they could look for the skills to make that family work.

Yet another skill has to do with recognizing the need for help and finding help for the family. The discipline of family therapy recognizes that an individual's problem may be an expression of family difficulties. This discipline also recognizes that this person's healing will be achieved in the family or not at all. Congregations need not offer family therapy themselves. They can help, however, by educating people to the fact that family therapists exist and encouraging people to seek such help when they need it.

The church that attempts even part of what we have briefly mentioned will not lack for curriculum or program ideas!

An Advocacy Task

Finally, caring planners have an advocacy task which is at least threefold.

The first part is advocacy with the church. As we contemplate this aspect, we are reminded of a sales manager's words to his sales force. He told them, "The best salesmanship you will ever have to do is with our own company employees—to persuade them to deliver the services and goods you sell to others. You will need to persuade people to deliver them complete, in good shape, and on time!"

Advocates for ministry with changing families may have a similar task with their churches. In the main, churches are conservative organizations. This quality has served them well in many ways. Conserving values, commitments, and structures that may be all too easily abandoned in a rapidly changing society has been a function of the church. Therefore, it may not be easy for a church itself to change and become a receptive community generating creative programs for changing families.

The family advocate may need to help the church see afresh what are the most central values it needs to conserve. Then perhaps there will be the discovery that changing families can benefit from these values as well. The church may well be an agent of stability for changing families. This gift, stability, might well be offered to a single-parent family in the form of support groups and whatever practical help is needed so that the parent can provide a good environment for the children. A remarried family may be struggling with the same issue—staying together amid the many-faceted frictions of early remarriage. The stability of supportive congregational life may be the factor that enables them to make it.

Advocates will discover ways to raise a church's consciousness and keep the variety of family types before the congregation. Here are half a dozen examples.

1. Some churches have a different family light the Advent candles each Sunday of Advent. These families could include a single-parent family, a remarried family, a childless couple, and an international family, for example.

2. Church membership lists can be checked for accuracy of names, including hyphenated names, international names, and multiple surnames. In children's records, all adults who might want to be informed about child-parent activities should be listed.

3. At family night programs, various families can share varied ethnic traditions about Easter, Thanksgiving, Christmas, and birthdays, as well as their special holidays or celebrations.

4. Advocates can remind nominating committees to include representatives of diverse family types on whatever board plans marriage and family programming in the church.

5. Advocates may need to remind program planners that with the rushed, changing schedules of so many persons, more events need to be planned to be complete in themselves. Advance notice of events, so that families with many obligations can participate, is most important. Catered meals rather than potluck meals may allow participation of busy two-career families.

6. Planners should remember that financial strain is a constant part of many family types. Planning with cost in mind and listing the cost of events graciously allows responsible decisions for families of limited means.

Such changes, as we have noted, may be not so much in the area of additional programming as in responsiveness to families in what is being done. This was Bob Rhymer's discovery.

> My approach to ministry has changed since my recent studies. I now seek to do ministry based on communicated needs and try to work within the limits of family structures and schedules. I'm not as concerned about attendance at church events as I am about how our ministry is impacting the lives of our people. My emphasis is upon being a part of a nurturing community rather than upon perfect attendance. This approach has caused me to:
>
> • Provide transportation after school for a youth whose parents both work, so he can attend youth fellowship.
> • Change our after-school youth meetings to Sunday afternoon because three of our seven regulars made the basketball team, which practices every day after school.
> • Spend more time with youth one on one.
> • Counsel with a single-parent family while providing youth group nurturing for siblings.
> • Allow youth to come late or leave early from special events such as lock-ins and retreats and service projects.

• Visit with parents in the home to affirm and seek input.

• Plan major events (retreats, summer trips) well in advance to help families in planning so that their youth can be involved.

• Bill myself as a pastor seeking to minister to families and individuals where they are, rather than a program coordinator who expects loyalty to a group of activities.

I receive a great deal of support from parents and youth, and, in fact, attendance and individual involvement is pretty good.

As these suggestions and samples show, the task of advocating on behalf of changing families with the church takes many forms and will never be completely finished.

The second part of the advocacy work will have to do with changing families. These families may have memories of churches that were not sensitive to them in an earlier time. There may be suspicion and hurt feelings. Interpretations of church positions and congregational values may need to be offered. It will be of help to indicate that, since not all church members are in the same place, no one member speaks for all. If one member makes an insensitive remark to a member of a changing family, that person does not speak for the whole church. Changing families may need to be recruited to the ongoing educative and advocacy tasks within the church.

At the same time, there is a third advocacy task. This one is to work with all those institutions and agencies whose policies and practices impact families. As the church attempts to create a more hospitable atmosphere for families, so should society. This will happen only if caring people make the needs visible and rally enough support so that agencies begin to change.

This task might begin with the changing families themselves. Parents may need to be empowered and informed as to their rights, responsibilities, and privileges as leaders of families. Families need to reclaim their role at the center of decision-making.

Family advocacy may be needed with employers for such issues as allowing both husband and wife to work for the same employer, flexible-time employment, day-care on the premises, and job training.

Family advocacy may be needed with local social service agencies, to help with measures that could expedite the process through which families wanting children and children needing permanent homes are brought together, for example.

Family advocacy may be needed with realtors and lending agencies to see that interracial-ethnic-cultural-national families are not discriminated against.

Family advocacy may be needed with state legislatures and the United States Congress. The issues raised by the needs of poverty-stricken families, including single-parent families, are many: affordable child care, nonpunitive welfare regulations, available student loans for persons from families of modest means are but a few of these issues. Prompt justice in cases of crime and therapy for crime victims is another. Homes for the homeless, food for the hungry, nursing home care and other services for the aged and infirm, protection of abused children and spouses—these and many other issues need caring advocates.

Again, this advocacy may be with mental health agencies, encouraging them to provide more family therapy support and to develop sensitivity to all kinds of families.

The advocacy tasks may be educative—for example, pressing for more family skills courses in public schools—or preventive—for example, helping to establish or support family planning clinics.

Throughout our discussion a central concept has been the power of the human relationship for good or evil. Therefore the family where the first relationship occurs and many relationships endure is of immeasurable importance. We have urged the sensitive nurture and support of families in the many forms in which they exist. As we have explored these family forms, we have discovered that too often our present society is not a hospitable place for all families. There is work to do!

We anticipate that congregations and church leaders will be creative, inventing a variety of responses to changing families and their needs. We are convinced that, both actually and potentially, the church is the best friend the family ever had!

Resources and References

Curran, Dolores. 1980. *Family: A Church Challenge for the 80s*. Minneapolis: Winston Press.

Durka, Gloria, and Joanmarie Smith, eds. 1980. *Family Ministry*. Minneapolis: Winston Press.

Guernsey, Dennis B. 1982. *A New Design for Family Ministry*. Elgin, Ill.: David C. Cook Publishing Co.

Larson, Jim. 1986. *A Church Guide for Strengthening Families*. Minneapolis: Augsburg Publishing House.

Leonard, Joe. 1982. *Planning Family Ministry*. Valley Forge, Pa.: Judson Press.

Mace, David, and Vera Mace. 1976. *Marriage Enrichment in the Church*. Nashville: Broadman Press.

Money, Royce. 1984. *Building Stronger Families*. Wheaton, Ill.: Victor Books.

———. 1987. *Ministering to Families: A Positive Plan of Action.* Abilene, Tex.: Abilene Christian University Press.

Sawin, Margaret M. 1979. *Family Enrichment with Family Clusters.* Valley Forge, Pa.: Judson Press.

Sell, Charles M. 1981. *Family Ministry: The Enrichment of Family Life Through the Church.* Grand Rapids: Zondervan Publishing House.